THE
SHAWNEE

Lake Superior

CANADA

Lake Michigan

MICHIGAN

Lake Huron

Huron

ONTARIO

Lake Ontario

Potawatomi

NEW

Iroquois

YORK

Detroit

Fort Malden →

Thames River

Lake Erie

Fort Miamis

PENNSYLVANIA

Fort Meigs

Cleveland

Delaware

Tippecanoe River

Maumee River

OHIO

Fort Pitt (Pittsburgh)

Prophetstown ▲

River

Wabash

Fort Greenville

Scioto River

Ohio River

Kickapoo

INDIANA

Fort Washington (Cincinnati)

Miami

SHAWNEE

Vincennes

Ohio River

WEST VIRGINIA

KENTUCKY

0   150 miles

INDIANS OF NORTH AMERICA

THE
SHAWNEE

Janet Hubbard-Brown

Frank W. Porter III
General Editor

CHELSEA HOUSE PUBLISHERS
New York   Philadelphia

On the cover   A beaded hair ornament worn by
Shawnee women during ceremonies.

Chelsea House Publishers
Editorial Director   Richard Rennert
Executive Managing Editor   Karyn Gullen Browne
Copy Chief   Robin James
Picture Editor   Adrian G. Allen
Art Director   Robert Mitchell
Manufacturing Director   Gerald Levine
Assistant Art Director   Joan Ferrigno

Indians of North America
Senior Editor   Sean Dolan
Native American Specialist   Jack Miller

Staff for **THE SHAWNEE**
Assistant Editor   Mary B. Sisson
Editorial Assistant   Annie McDonnell
Designer   John Infantino
Picture Researcher   Sandy Jones

3   5   7   9   8   6   4   2

Library of Congress Cataloging-in-Publication Data

Hubbard-Brown, Janet.
    The Shawnee / Janet Hubbard-Brown.
       p.   cm.—(Indians of North America)
    Includes bibliographical references and index.
    ISBN 0-7910-1686-2
    1. Shawnee Indians—History—Juvenile
literature. [1. Shawnee Indians. 2. Indians of North
America.] I. Title. II. Series: Indians of North America
(Chelsea House Publishers)
E99.S35H83   1995   94-29006
973'.04973—dc20   CIP
                                               AC

CONTENTS

INDIANS OF NORTH AMERICA

CHELSEA HOUSE PUBLISHERS

INDIANS OF NORTH AMERICA: CONFLICT AND SURVIVAL

Frank W. Porter III

The Indians survived our open intention of wiping them out, and since the tide turned they have even weathered our good intentions toward them, which can be much more deadly.

John Steinbeck
America and Americans

When Europeans first reached the North American continent, they found hundreds of tribes occupying a vast and rich country. The newcomers quickly recognized the wealth of natural resources. They were not, however, so quick or willing to recognize the spiritual, cultural, and intellectual riches of the people they called Indians.

The Indians of North America examines the problems that develop when people with different cultures come together. For American Indians, the consequences of their interaction with non-Indian people have been both productive and tragic. The Europeans believed they had "discovered" a "New World," but their religious bigotry, cultural bias, and materialistic world view kept them from appreciating and understanding the people who lived in it. All too often they attempted to change the way of life of the indigenous people. The Spanish conquistadores wanted the Indians as a source of labor. The Christian missionaries, many of whom were English, viewed them as potential converts. French traders and trappers used the Indians as a means to obtain pelts. As Francis Parkman, the 19th-century historian, stated, "Spanish civilization crushed the Indian; English civilization scorned and neglected him; French civilization embraced and cherished him."

7

Nearly 500 years later, many people think of American Indians as curious vestiges of a distant past, waging a futile war to survive in a Space Age society. Even today, our understanding of the history and culture of American Indians is too often derived from unsympathetic, culturally biased, and inaccurate reports. The American Indian, described and portrayed in thousands of movies, television programs, books, articles, and government studies, has either been raised to the status of the "noble savage" or disparaged as the "wild Indian" who resisted the westward expansion of the American frontier.

Where in this popular view are the real Indians, the human beings and communities whose ancestors can be traced back to ice-age hunters? Where are the creative and indomitable people whose sophisticated technologies used the natural resources to ensure their survival, whose military skill might even have prevented European settlement of North America if not for devastating epidemics and disruption of the ecology? Where are the men and women who are today diligently struggling to assert their legal rights and express once again the value of their heritage?

The various Indian tribes of North America, like people everywhere, have a history that includes population expansion, adaptation to a range of regional environments, trade across wide networks, internal strife, and warfare. This was the reality. Europeans justified their conquests, however, by creating a mythical image of the New World and its native people. In this myth, the New World was a virgin land, waiting for the Europeans. The arrival of Christopher Columbus ended a timeless primitiveness for the original inhabitants.

Also part of this myth was the debate over the origins of the American Indians. Fantastic and diverse answers were proposed by the early explorers, missionairies, and settlers. Some thought that the Indians were descended from the Ten Lost Tribes of Israel, others that they were descended from inhabitants of the lost continent of Atlantis. One writer suggested that the Indians had reached North America in another Noah's ark.

A later myth, perpetrated by many historians, focused on the relentless persecution during the past five centuries until only a scattering of these "primitive" people remained to be herded onto reservations. This view fails to chronicle the overt and covert ways in which the Indians successfully coped with the intruders.

All of these myths presented one-sided interpretations that ignored the complexity of European and American events and policies. All left serious questions unanswered. What were the origins of the American Indians? Where did they come from? How and when did they get to the New World? What was their life—their culture—really like?

In the late 1800s, anthropologists and archaeologists in the Smithsonian Institution's newly created Bureau of American Ethnology in Washington,

D.C., began to study scientifically the history and culture of the Indians of North America. They were motivated by an honest belief that the Indians were on the verge of extinction and that along with them would vanish their languages, religious beliefs, technology, myths, and legends. These men and women went out to visit, study, and record data from as many Indian communities as possible before this information was forever lost.

By this time there was a new myth in the national consciousness. American Indians existed as figures in the American past. They had performed a historical mission. They had challenged white settlers who trekked across the continent. Once conquered, however, they were supposed to accept graciously the way of life of their conquerors.

The reality again was different. American Indians resisted both actively and passively. They refused to lose their unique identity, to be assimilated into white society. Many whites viewed the Indians not only as members of a conquered nation but also as "inferior" and "unequal." The rights of the Indians could be expanded, contracted, or modified as the conquerors saw fit. In every generation, white society asked itself what to do with the American Indians. Their answers have resulted in the twists and turns of federal Indian policy.

There were two general approaches. One way was to raise the Indians to a "higher level" by "civilizing" them. Zealous missionaries considered it their Christian duty to elevate the Indian through conversion and scanty education. The other approach was to ignore the Indians until they disappeared under pressure from the ever-expanding white society. The myth of the "vanishing Indian" gave stronger support to the latter option, helping to justify the taking of the Indians' land.

Prior to the end of the 18th century, there was no national policy on Indians simply because the American nation had not yet come into existence. American Indians similarly did not possess a political or social unity with which to confront the various Europeans. They were not homogeneous. Rather, they were loosely formed bands and tribes, speaking nearly 300 languages and thousands of dialects. The collective identity felt by Indians today is a result of their common experiences of defeat and/or mistreatment at the hands of whites.

During the colonial period, the British crown did not have a coordinated policy toward the Indians of North America. Specific tribes (most notably the Iroquois and the Cherokee) became military and political pawns used by both the crown and the individual colonies. The success of the American Revolution brought no immediate change. When the United States acquired new territory from France and Mexico in the early 19th century, the federal government wanted to open this land to settlement by homesteaders. But the Indian tribes that lived on this land had signed treaties with European governments assuring their title to the land. Now the United States assumed legal responsibility for honoring these treaties.

At first, President Thomas Jefferson believed that the Louisiana Purchase contained sufficient land for both the Indians and the white population. Within a generation, though, it became clear that the Indians would not be allowed to remain. In the 1830s the federal government began to coerce the eastern tribes to sign treaties agreeing to relinquish their ancestral land and move west of the Mississippi River. Whenever these negotiations failed, President Andrew Jackson used the military to remove the Indians. The southeastern tribes, promised food and transportation during their removal to the West, were instead forced to walk the "Trail of Tears." More than 4,000 men, woman, and children died during this forced march. The "removal policy" was successful in opening the land to homesteaders, but it created enormous hardships for the Indians.

By 1871 most of the tribes in the United States had signed treaties ceding most or all of their ancestral land in exchange for reservations and welfare. The treaty terms were intended to bind both parties for all time. But in the General Allotment Act of 1887, the federal government changed its policy again. Now the goal was to make tribal members into individual landowners and farmers, encouraging their absorption into white society. This policy was advantageous to whites who were eager to acquire Indian land, but it proved disastrous for the Indians. One hundred thirty-eight million acres of reservation land were subdivided into tracts of 160, 80, or as little as 40 acres, and allotted tribe members on an individual basis. Land owned in this way was said to have "trust status" and could not be sold. But the surplus land—all Indian land not allotted to individuals—was opened (for sale) to white settlers. Ultimately, more than 90 million acres of land were taken from the Indians by legal and illegal means.

The resulting loss of land was a catastrophe for the Indians. It was necessary to make it illegal for Indians to sell their land to non-Indians. The Indian Reorganization Act of 1934 officially ended the allotment period. Tribes that voted to accept the provisions of this act were reorganized, and an effort was made to purchase land within preexisting reservations to restore an adequate land base.

Ten years later, in 1944, federal Indian policy again shifted. Now the federal government wanted to get out of the "Indian business." In 1953 an act of Congress named specific tribes whose trust status was to be ended "at the earliest possible time." This new law enabled the United States to end unilaterally, whether the Indians wished it or not, the special status that protected the land in Indian tribal reservations. In the 1950s federal Indian policy was to transfer federal responsibility and jurisdiction to state governments, encourage the physical relocation of Indian peoples from reservations to urban areas, and hasten the termination, or extinction, of tribes.

Between 1954 and 1962 Congress passed specific laws authorizing the termination of more than 100 tribal groups. The stated purpose of the termination policy was to ensure the full and complete integration of Indians into American society. However, there is a less benign way to interpret this legislation. Even as termination was being discussed in Congress, 133 separate bills were introduced to permit the transfer of trust land ownership from Indians to non-Indians.

With the Johnson administration in the 1960s the federal government began to reject termination. In the 1970s yet another Indian policy emerged. Known as "self-determination," it favored keeping the protective role of the federal government while increasing tribal participation in, and control of, important areas of local government. In 1983 President Reagan, in a policy statement on Indian affairs, restated the unique "government is government" relationship of the United States with the Indians. However, federal programs since then have moved toward transferring Indian affairs to individual states, which have long desired to gain control of Indian land and resources.

As long as American Indians retain power, land, and resources that are coveted by the states and the federal government, there will continue to be a "clash of cultures," and the issues will be contested in the courts, Congress, the White House, and even in the international human rights community. To give all Americans a greater comprehension of the issues and conflicts involving American Indians today is a major goal of this series. These issues are not easily understood, nor can these conflicts be readily resolved. The study of North American Indian history and culture is a necessary and important step toward that comprehension. All Americans must learn the history of the relations between the Indians and the federal government, recognize the unique legal status of the Indians, and understand the heritage and cultures of the Indians of North America.

This 1796 drawing, made by a traveling artist in what is now Illinois, portrays a Shawnee man holding a bow and arrows. Although the original homeland of the Shawnees remains unknown, by the 18th century they had established a strong presence in the Ohio River valley and surrounding area.

UNCERTAIN ORIGINS

The origins of the Shawnees, the people who once inhabited Kentucky and the Ohio River valley, are veiled in mystery. The Shawnees moved into the area surrounding the Ohio River and its tributaries fairly recently in their history, after contact with the Europeans had been made, and the question of what area they inhabited previously has long been a matter of contention, being variously placed by anthropologists and archaeologists in the Northeast, the Southeast, and the prairie region of the United States. The only aspect of the Shawnees' early history that is absolutely certain is that they were a migratory people—indeed, it has been claimed that no other tribe has moved, divided, and reunited more times than the Shawnees. Bands and subtribes of Shawnees wandered

through the midwestern prairies and southeastern mountains for centuries, erecting temporary villages, then abandoning them for any number of reasons.

Despite the dearth of historical information on the early Shawnees, the Shawnee language bears similarities to those of the Delawares, Miamis, Illinois, Blackfeet, Cheyennes, Sacs, Foxes, Kickapoos, and other tribes grouped together by linguists as the Central Algonquins. This grouping, however useful to historians, who view linguistic similarities between groups as indications of a shared origin, does not reflect any political alliance or sense of unity among the Central Algonquin tribes themselves; not only did the Shawnees war with many of those tribes, but present-day Shawnees are often quite surprised at the similarity of their speech to that of other Algonquin tribes, with whom for the most part they feel no close cultural bond. In the Algonquian language, the name for the Shawnees is *Shawunogi,* meaning "Southerners," perhaps indicating that at one time the Shawnees inhabited an area further south than the other Algonquin tribes. Many of the approximately 150 names and spellings used by various people over the years to refer to the Shawnees are variants on this word; the English colonists initially referred to them as the Savanas, then the Shawanos, and finally, the Shawnees.

The Algonquins—including, presumably, the Shawnees—originated somewhere in the eastern subarctic area of Canada, probably near Lake Winnipeg. A Delaware migration legend has the Shawnees leaving Canada around A.D. 1240 and perhaps passing through the Great Lakes area around A.D. 1500. The Delaware and Shawnee tribes have a significant shared history, and one legend claims that the two tribes were once united—but split due to a children's quarrel over the possession of a grasshopper. Accepting this legend as evidence that the Shawnees and Delawares are in fact one tribe is questionable, however, since another legend, attributed to the Sacs in some sources and the Kickapoos in others, maintains that the Shawnees were in fact united with either the Sacs or the Kickapoos, but split over a hunter's quarrel about the division of some roasted bear paws.

In any case, reports from early European expeditions in North America suggest that the Shawnees were probably a part of the prehistoric Fort Ancient culture, which dates from A.D. 1000 to 1650 and occupied the area of southern Ohio, southern Indiana, northern Kentucky, and western West Virginia. The Fort Ancient people combined hunting, fishing, and gathering with some agriculture, using digging sticks to plant fields of corn, squash, beans, and sunflowers. They built rectangular or circular houses made of poles covered with bark or mats of split cattails, and their villages were laid out in a circular manner, usually near rivers, and were stockaded. Tools of the Fort Ancient culture were made of chipped stone, bone, shell, and pottery, and their weapons included the bow and arrow. Although some European goods have been found in the ruins of some Fort Ancient villages, they are thought to have been obtained through trade with other Indian tribes and not through any direct contact with the Europeans.

Unfortunately, Shawnee oral history does not greatly aid in the question of their origins. In part, this is because the spoken historical narratives of the Shawnees changed with each storyteller and often reflected contemporary concerns as much as past events. In addition, while Shawnee mythology shares many similarities to those of other Algonquin tribes, it departs radically in important details. For example, the Shawnee creation myth is similar to other Algonquin creation myths in maintaining that the people who are now the Shawnees originated from a different world—an island balanced on the back of a giant turtle—

Archaeologists and laborers pose with their shovels next to an excavation of a Fort Ancient burial site in Scioto County, Ohio. The theory that the Shawnees are descended from the Fort Ancient people has generated a good deal of controversy in recent years as Shawnee proponents have attempted to reclaim Fort Ancient sites.

and traveled to this one. The myth quickly departs from the norm, however. According to Shawnee myth, when the first people were on the island, they could see nothing but water, which they did not know how to cross. They prayed for aid and were miraculously transported across the water. The Shawnees are the only Algonquin tribe whose creation story includes the passage of their ancestors over the sea, and for many years they held an annual sacrifice in thanks of the safe arrival of their ancestors in this country.

The Shawnees are also unique among Algonquin peoples in believing their creator was a woman, who they call Kokumthena, which means "Our Grandmother." Kokumthena is usually depicted as an anthropomorphic female with gray hair whose size ranges from gigantic to very small. According to Shawnee myth, the idea of creation came from the Great Spirit, who is called Moneto, but the actual work of creation was performed by Kokumthena, and she is the most important figure in Shawnee religion. She lives in a home in the sky and, in addition to Shawnee and other Native American languages, speaks her own non-Shawnee language that can only be understood by children under age four—who forget it as soon as they begin to learn Shawnee.

In addition to creating the world, Kokumthena will end it. Prophets who travel to the afterworld find her weaving a net, but she has a little dog who unravels what she has done during the night. Someday, however, she will complete

her net, scoop up the virtuous to come live with her, and punish and destroy the wicked. This belief in a female creator/destroyer probably surfaced in or after 1824, although it may have existed earlier, and there are mixed opinions among historians about the reasons behind the emergence of this belief. Some believe that Kokumthena was inspired by a female deity of the Iroquois named Ataentsic, while another theory holds that the story of the Virgin Mary in Christian mythology influenced Shawnee myth.

In any case, the existing versions of the Kokumthena myth reflect past and current tensions between the Shawnees and the Europeans. Kokumthena's country resembles this earth but is without whites, and the dead as well as the living participating in ceremonies must wear Shawnee paint and costume so that Kokumthena will not mistake them for whites on the day she completes her net. The Shawnee creation myth also contains warnings of a great white spirit who will try to change the creator's designs and shorten the years of the Shawnees and warnings of a great serpent who will come from the seas and destroy the Shawnees. According to Shawnee oral tradition, when the Shawnees first saw European ships, they recognized the forked ends of the Europeans' pennants as symbols of the tongue of the serpent.

The Shawnees also had their share of conflict with other Native American tribes. In part, this was due to their nomadic wanderings, which encroached

*This 1820 watercolor by Fleury Generelly shows a Shawnee temporary camp along
the Mississippi River. The numbers label (1) a pole-and-bark shelter, (2) an infant's hammock,
(3) a mortar for grinding corn hollowed from a log, and (4) a deerskin stretched for drying.*

on the territory of other tribes. A larger part was played, however, by their willingness to hire out to other tribes as warriors in exchange for the temporary use of hunting land. (One writer even labeled them "traveling mercenaries.") Usually the hunting land they received would be in disputed territory, and the Shawnees would form a buffer between the two hostile nations.

By the early 17th century, the Shawnees had gained a new, determined enemy, the Iroquois Confederation. Hostility between the Iroquois and Shawnee had escalated through the years as the Iroquois, based in the eastern Great Lakes area, continued their push to dominate the other tribes in the Northeast. Iroquois aggression was motivated by their need to impress their

European allies, the British, with their influence and control of other Native American tribes and to wrest control of the highly lucrative fur trade from their European and Native American rivals, the French and the Hurons. The Iroquois expansion was the first in a long string of hostilities in the Old Northwest marked by self-serving alliances between various European nations and the many Native American tribes—alliances that would drastically affect Shawnee history.

The Shawnees first became known to Europeans around 1670, through reports by other tribes made to French explorers. At this time, they had a population of approximately 10,000 to 12,000 people. The Shawnee were at this time living in two main bodies: one in the Cumberland region of Tennessee, and the other on the Savannah River in South Carolina. In 1673, two French explorers, Louis Jolliet and Jacques Marquette, made a journal entry when they passed the mouth of the Ohio River, stating, "This river flows from the lands of the East, where dwell the people called Chaouanons [Shawnees] in so great numbers that in one district there are as many as 23 villages, and 15 in another, quite near one another. They are not at all warlike, and are the nations whom the Iroquois go so far to seek, and war against without any reason."

As Jolliet and Marquette's journal entry implies, hostilities between the Iroquois and the Shawnees continued through the 1670s. The Iroquois repeatedly attacked the Shawnees in the Ohio

Valley until they began to disperse, breaking into small bands and spreading out in order to save themselves. A few hundred Shawnees went to Starved Rock on the Illinois River, while others moved into the Southeast near what is now Augusta, Georgia, and became a dominant tribe there. Western Virginia became home to a few bands, and others either stayed in the Ohio Valley or went north into the territories of the Miamis and the Illinois on Lake Michigan. (The ever-thorough Iroquois attacked the Miamis in 1684 as a result of this last migration.) This dispersal tactic was commonly followed by the Shawnees when they were threatened, being a sort of logical extension of their normal nomadic existence. Because they had protected many tribes from enemies in the past, they had good relations with a number of tribes and moved easily from one tribe's territory to that of another. (Despite Jolliet and Marquette's claim that the Shawnees were "not at all warlike," they were well-respected warriors.)

In 1690, the Delawares gave the Shawnees a grant of land in the Ohio Valley. The land, being both familiar and relatively uncontested, attracted many of the roving bands of Shawnees, and soon more Shawnees were gathered there than had ever lived together before. When the Iroquois visited the area in the 1690s, they discovered that not only had many of the Shawnees whom they had expelled had returned, but that the hated French had also moved in. Predictably, the Iroquois

This 1936 painting by Seneca artist Ernest Smith depicts the creation of the Iroquois Confederation, a powerful alliance of five (later six) separate tribes. Although member tribes swore to be at peace with one another, no such promise was made to tribes outside the coalition, and the Iroquois proved formidable foes to the Shawnees.

Native Americans wage war in canoes in this drawing. Conflicts over hunting territory became increasingly common during the 17th century as newly opened European markets made the fur trade more and more lucrative.

launched a number of attacks against the Shawnees and the Miamis (who also lived in the area), but the attacks were unsuccessful, and the Iroquois withdrew their war parties.

After their campaign against the Shawnees, the Iroquois declared to all who would listen that their western adventures had been a huge success and that the Ohio Valley nations were now their vassals. They called themselves the "Heads and Superiors of all Indian nations of the Continent of America." It was an outrageous claim, but the British were quick to respect it, more out of shrewdness than ignorance. The Iroquois were closely allied with the British and willing to help them expand their American empire (provided they did not attempt to take Iroquois land), while the Ohio Valley nations were closer to the French, who were competing with the

British for American territory and resources. Consequently, the British were quite willing to accept the Iroquois' word over that of the Ohio Valley tribes and went so far as to claim the Iroquois "empire" as a client state, a relationship that according to European law gave Britain legal title to all territories the Iroquois League claimed it owned by right of conquest. In exchange for turning over lands they did not own to the British, the Iroquois received cash, long-term subsidies, special trading privileges, and most importantly, European guns and ammunition.

While the Iroquois were declaring themselves the conquerors of the west, a group of Shawnees were migrating east. In 1707, some Shawnees moved to Pennsylvania and founded Lower Shawnee Town, located on the mouth of the Scioto River, which became a major Shawnee center in the early 18th century and an important post for English and French fur traders. The Iroquois were not pleased by this incursion by a supposedly conquered people. They continued to insist they were the overlords of the Shawnees, and colonial authorities once again found it convenient to deal with the Shawnees and other western tribes through the Iroquois. The Shawnees responded by flatly ignoring agreements made by the Iroquois whenever possible. Things reached a head when the Pennsylvanian Shawnees began to expand their fur trading operations to the west in violation of an agreement made between the Iroquois and the colonists. Colonial authorities

demanded that the Iroquois retrieve the traders. The Iroquois sent a delegation in 1735 to negotiate a return with some of the Shawnee trading bands, but a member of the Iroquois party was killed by the Shawnees, dealing a significant blow to Iroquois prestige and authority in the eyes of the Europeans.

Iroquois hostility, however onerous, proved to be of much less consequence to the Shawnees than the increase in the European population of North America. The white population in what is now the United States soared from 250,000 people in 1700 to 1.5 million in 1760, and a new influx of German and Scotch-Irish immigrants headed to the seemingly plentiful lands to the west, away from the English-dominated, increasingly crowded eastern coastline. The British government, concerned that the new settlers would interfere with the fur trade, tried to control the flood of immigrants, but the determination of the settlers made this task difficult. The Ohio Valley tribes had dealt with European traders and European diseases (which would kill thousands of them long before armed conflict erupted), but the settlers were a unique threat. Unlike traders, settlers were primarily interested in taking Native American land—and they were willing to fight for it.

The European settlers and the Native Americans had two extremely different philosophies toward the use of land, and neither fully appreciated at the time how incompatible these philosophies were. Although the eastern woodlands of the United States had been occupied for at

*This aged Shawnee chief, named Goes up the River, was painted by noted artist
George Catlin (1796–1872). He wears a nose ring and a buffalo robe, and his ear rims
have been distended—three of the many traditional Shawnee practices that were
considered savage and barbaric by Europeans.*

least 10,000 years and various nations had established territorial rights, ownership of land by individuals was a foreign concept to the Native Americans. The Native Americans did not use the land as intently as Europeans, therefore it did not need to be managed in the same way. Their economy was based on foraging and hunting that harvested natural surpluses, which meant they required a great deal of unspoiled land. Although, like the Europeans, the Native Americans farmed, unlike the Europeans they did so for only a few months each year, did not keep domestic animals, and did not do anything to keep the land fertile, simply moving on when the soil became depleted. In contrast, the European agricultural economy was based on private farms, where one family would stay on one small plot of land possibly for generations. Intense land management was necessary to keep farmland fertile and productive; in addition, the European economy relied a great deal on manufacture and commerce, both activities requiring extensive infrastructure that, like the farms, destroyed the wilderness the Native Americans needed to survive. When the Europeans saw Indian land, they saw land that was, in their minds, not being used at all; when the Native Americans saw European farming techniques, they saw the devastation and rape of formerly productive land.

As the British settlers spread slowly but surely west, competition developed between the French and the British for land in and around the Ohio Valley, and in the mid-1700s, the French colonial government began to encourage Indian raids on British settlements. There was, however, little love between the French and the Shawnees at this point, and most Shawnees simply avoided the whites as much as possible. Their traditional lifestyle sustained them well, and the Shawnees were probably as well or better off during this period than many of their white contemporaries who were struggling to sustain themselves in cities in Europe and on the East Coast of North America. ▲

An Algonquin priest-shaman performs a ritual chant while preparing a mixture. The Shawnees had a well-functioning, complex society that operated under the guidance of a variety of civil and religious leaders, but it was strained almost to the breaking point by the enormous influx of European settlers.

2

TO
BE
SHAWNEE

By the early 18th century, contact between the Shawnees and the Europeans was fairly common, and a good deal of information exists on Shawnee life during this period. The Shawnee population had been reduced through disease and warfare to approximately 3,000 to 4,000 people, and most Shawnees now lived in the Ohio Valley area, but despite the contact with Europeans, the reduction in population, and the shift to a more settled existence, traditional Shawnee life and culture was very much in evidence.

Perhaps the most important thing that happened to an individual in Shawnee society—indeed, the thing that made a newborn considered an actual human being—was the naming ceremony, arranged by the parents shortly after a Shawnee child was born. During the naming ceremony (which has survived to this day), two people—not necessarily relatives—chosen by the parents to name the child prayed for a name. When the name appeared in a dream or came to mind, the name givers determined which name group the name belonged to (name groups were nonfamilial associations of people linked by their names). On the 10th morning after the birth of the child, the mother—who had been held in seclusion—emerged, and a special ceremony was held to name the child. The name givers told the parents the names they had selected for the child, being sure to offer two names from different name groups so the parents would have some control over the child's affiliation. If the parents disagreed on the name, the mother made the final decision. The father gave a name giver a string of white beads, which were eventually tied around the baby's neck and worn until the string broke. Everyone had a breakfast prepared by the female relatives of the child, during which a taste of all the foods was put on the baby's tongue. If the child turned out to be sickly, a name-changing ceremony would follow. A name-changing ceremony was also organized if the name givers had mistakenly given the infant a name that someone else already had, because of the belief that sharing a name was quite dangerous—if one person died, there was a good chance that their namesake would also die.

The Shawnees trained their children early on in the strong moral code that existed within the tribe, teaching them to be supportive of and absolutely honest toward other tribe members. Children were rarely threatened or physically punished, and using a stick to beat a child was considered a disgrace both for the child and for the parent. Instead, parents and other adults appealed to the child's pride, and a few words of praise from an adult was considered the highest prize for good behavior. A parent would punish a child by shaming him, telling a visitor or friend the child's faults in front of the child.

Shawnee children learned self-control and how to conceal their feelings very early in life—important skills in Shawnee society, as any kind of noise or the wrong movement could spoil a hunt

or alert an enemy. Babies were fed before they began to cry for food; if they did begin to cry, they were picked up and cradled to make them stop. Infants were strapped to a cradle board from the age of one month until they could sit up by themselves, a custom that the Shawnees believed would make the child grow straight and strong (it also produced a flat spot on the backs of their heads), and they were bathed daily in cold water to make them hardy.

Older children learned by doing, with fathers instructing sons and mothers instructing daughters, who learned necessary skills such as weaving baskets and tanning hides by imitating their mothers and other women in the tribe. Both boys and girls spent a lot of time with the elderly of the tribe, who fulfilled the role of teachers. Girls and boys were rarely allowed to play together, but both played games engineered to develop strength, skill, and resourcefulness. Children wrestled, fished, hunted, ran races, and played games similar to marbles and lacrosse. A popular boy's game was the hoop and pole game. A hoop was made of grapevine, and the inside was filled with netting of pliable bark. The boys chose sides and stood in two lines, facing each other approximately 15 or 20 feet apart. A boy from one side would roll the hoop along, and the boys on the opposite side would shoot at it with their bows and arrows as it went by. The boy whose arrow stuck in the netting was the winner.

When Shawnee boys reached age nine, they began a special program of

A Native American woman carries her child and a load of fuel in this drawing. Although children in Shawnee culture were rarely punished physically, they were not coddled but instead taught at an early age how to provide for the tribe.

training to increase endurance and self-control. One such exercise was to take early morning dips in the cold water of a pond or lake, breaking the ice that had formed the night before if necessary. Around the time of puberty, boys were sent out into the woods to fast and to seek a spirit helper. They would blacken their faces with charcoal, to indicate that they were not to be offered food or spoken to. The spirit helper would usually come to the seeker in the form of an animal or bird and would give the seeker some kind of instruction that would protect them and help them in life. A Shawnee boy could bear arms by age 15, but young men were still considered under the control of adults until age 20 and generally married in their mid or late twenties.

Girls did not undergo special training to become warriors (although women could and did fight in battles), and they usually married at a much younger age, around 16. Shawnee marriages were usually arranged by the parents, and children could not marry without their parents' consent. Ordinarily, a young man's parents would select a girl for him and make up a present of hides and other treasures for the girl's family, which the young man's mother would carry to the girl's mother. If the potential bride's family decided to accept the offer, they would divide the goods among the female relatives of the girl who, in turn, would cook a large quantity of vegetables and carry them to the home or village of the young man, accompanied by the bride-to-be and her

parents. The groom's friends would come, and everyone would celebrate, after which the bride was left with her husband, and they were considered married. Although adultery was strictly prohibited, couples could separate and remarry. Polygamy was occasionally practiced, but it became less popular as the 18th century went on.

Unlike Shawnee weddings, Shawnee funeral services were usually lengthy vigils that included songs, ceremonial dances, and speeches recollecting and honoring the deceased's life. Bodies of tribe members were always buried uncremated, most commonly in an east-west orientation, and great efforts were made to retrieve the corpses of warriors after battles, as it was considered highly disrespectful to leave a body unburied. Corpses were commonly wrapped in skins and placed in coffins made of tree bark, and items such as jewelry, tobacco, and cut strips of the last clothing worn by the deceased in health were placed on the coffin. The earliest existing account of a Shawnee funeral was written by a French explorer in 1687, who felt that the service, marked by singing and dancing and ending with a stick game to determine who would receive the goods left over from the funeral, was quite a cheerful one, although he may not have been aware of the serious religious nature of Shawnee song and dance. The explorer also claimed that the Shawnees buried the body along with some wheat and a pot in which to boil it in case the deceased felt hungry on his journey to the afterworld, a practice that

This young Shawnee man, called Straight Man, was painted in 1830 by George Catlin. Catlin dedicated his life to painting Indians in both North and South America, and his portraits are important records of Native American life at the time.

may have been unique to that particular band or time since later accounts make no mention of it.

Shawnee society had a very loose political structure, but it was organized into five patrilinear divisions: the Chalaakaatha, Mekoche, Thawikila, Pekowi, and Kishpoko. The names of these divisions may have been derived from the names of villages at a time when all the Shawnees were living in a common territory. Each division had its special function: the Pekowi division was in charge of anything pertaining to religion, and especially ceremonies; the Kishpoko was responsible for matters relating to war and the training of warriors; the Mekoche was in charge of health, healing, and food; and the Thawikila and Chalaakaatha—the two dominant divisions—were in control of all political affairs. The principal chief, who ruled over all the Shawnees, always came from the Thawikila or Chalaakaatha division, while the other three divisions had their own chiefs who were independent in making decisions affecting their division, but subordinate in larger issues to the principal chief. Despite this specialization, each of the five divisions had its own political, religious, and military unit; this autonomy, combined with the Shawnees characteristic mobility, resulted in a tribal authority that can best be described as loose.

Each division had its own name groups, and each person was assigned to a name group when they received their name. Name groups were believed to affect a person's personality or nature, as well as establish a supernatural link between the animals associated with a group and the people in that group. The name groups themselves were named after specific animals such as turtle, wolf, rabbit, bear, snake, or turkey, but despite their names, the groups usually included more than one creature—for example, the turkey name group would include all birds. Name groups provided an opportunity for a lot of good-natured teasing between members of various name groups—a member of the turtle group might be teased for being slow, for instance—but the Shawnees believed that a genuine emotional bond existed between members of a name group and between the members and the animal with which the group was associated. Each person's group affiliation was reflected in their name; for example, the name of the famous Shawnee warrior Tecumseh means "The Panther Passing Across," indicating that he belonged to the name group that encompassed all round-footed animals such as cats and dogs. While Shawnee society was politically grouped along the lines of divisions or village bands rather than along the lines of name groups, a person's name group was believed to have tremendous significance in their spiritual life and their personal destiny.

Shawnee divisions and isolated bands were led by both peace and war chiefs, as was common among the Algonquins. The position of peace chief was hereditary—unless the heir was deemed incapable, in which case the title passed to another family. The peace

Although Shawnee men were famous for their prowess in warfare, their skill at hunting was ultimately more important for their day-to-day survival. Here, Native American men spear fish at night with the help of torches, a common practice among the tribes of the Ohio Valley.

chief's responsibilities included organizing rituals and appointing people to ritual offices. The war chief, in contrast, earned his title by proving himself to be an exceptional warrior. War could not be declared unless the peace chiefs agreed to it, and war chiefs were not allowed a strong voice in civic matters, although they were involved in any intertribal affairs or decisions having to do with territory. There were also female war chiefs and peace chiefs, usually close relatives of the male chiefs, and they had a strong voice in tribal government. Widows of deceased male chiefs often stepped to their husband's position until a new chief was appointed.

If both war chiefs and peace chiefs agreed to declare war, the war chief would call upon members of his clan to "raise the tomahawk," and tribes allied with the Shawnees were sent a tomahawk painted with red clay as an invitation to join the war. Before the departure of the warriors, a war dance was performed, and a priest-shaman would bring out the division's sacred bundle, or *mishaami*, which contained holy objects considered extremely important to the success of the attack. Sometimes a female priest-shaman, usually an elderly woman, would be called in, and she would seclude herself to chant and make magic. The male priest-shaman would open the mishaami before the impending battle and hand out certain objects from it to members of the war party to wear for good luck. Then the leader would announce his plan of attack, and the warriors would set off at a trot in single file toward enemy territory. The war chief went ahead, singing the war march.

Chiefs also served as judges but usually only concerned themselves with offenses of a criminal nature, appointing others to take care of lesser matters. The word of the chief was law, and any refusal to obey the Shawnee's unwritten code of honorable behavior was punishable by a severe beating or death. (There were no jails.) Anyone who refused to accept the punishment for a crime was ostracized, a punishment considered worse than death. The Shawnee code differed from the European criminal codes at this time in that support for fellow tribe members, rather than respect for property, was paramount. For example, deceitfulness or slanderous gossip among Shawnee tribe members was considered a crime, but nonpayment of debts was not. (If a person did not pay a debt, however, the creditor was allowed to come in and take whatever property would make up the debt.) Thieves were given three chances to reform themselves, but if a person stole a fourth time, he was tied to a post and whipped. If the thievery continued, the thief's fate was put in the hands of those he had stolen from—ordinarily the victim would ambush and shoot the thief.

Murder could be rectified by a payment of blood money to the victim's family or by the death of the murderer at the hands of a member of the victim's family. If the murderer was popular and respected, the chiefs would try to help him secure the money and gifts to pay for the life of the victim. The chiefs would also let the victim's relatives know how much blood money was being raised, but the family was under no obligation to accept the gifts and could choose to kill the murderer instead. If the family preferred retribution to blood money, the chiefs warned the murderer. If the murderer was an unpopular person, the chiefs would either make no attempt to buy off the family or would deliver the murderer to the family of the slain person: a relative would kill the murderer, and the score would be considered even. It was considered a far greater crime to kill a woman than a man, and women were never executed for killing men, although they did have to pay blood money.

While chiefs acted as judges, lawmakers, and diplomats in Shawnee society, priest-shamans played the equally important and prestigious roles of healers, counselors, and diviners. Religious ceremonies, prescribed and led by the priest-shamans, played a tremendous role in Shawnee life, and rituals surrounded everything from spring planting to making war. All of the major ceremonies of the Shawnees (except for recent imports from other tribes, such as peyote rituals) were and are believed to have originated with Kokumthena. The

Shawnees also were great believers in magic and used it in many aspects of their lives, giving them a reputation among other tribes as a nation of wonder-workers.

Among the most important objects in Shawnee religion were the sacred bundles, called mishaami. Each division had its own bundle, which was believed to literally contain the welfare of not only the division or the tribe but the entire universe. In addition, people sometimes had their own personal sacred bundles that protected them and enabled them to cast spells. The mishaami also appear in the religious traditions of the Sacs, Foxes, and Kickapoos, and their history would probably reveal a great deal about the roots of these Native American religions; however, the rituals, contents, and history of the mishaami are considered sacred mysteries and are kept in secrecy even to this day. According to Shawnee legend, all the mishaami were given to the Shawnees by Kokumthena, who can still control them and will inform a chosen prophet if she desires a change in either the contents of a bundle or a ritual surrounding a bundle. Sacred bundles were usually kept in a special building and were regarded and treated much like human beings—one Shawnee chief recalled being sent as a child to rearrange the bundles once a month to keep them from getting cramped and uncomfortable (although children were generally kept away from such powerful magical objects). A custodian—always a man, and one of very high moral character—

was assigned to the mishaami by a division chief. The mishaami were consulted by the custodian whenever the tribe was considering a major move, and they were opened and their contents moved around before events such as battles in order to predict their outcome.

When not on the move, the Shawnees lived in villages that consisted of a council house (called a *msikamelwi*) usually surrounded closely by the *wegiwas*, or houses, of the chiefs and the priest-shamans. The homes of ordinary tribe members were further from the msikamelwi and radiated out in all directions, and the village itself was surrounded by cultivated fields.

Msikamelwis were large buildings (some could seat over 200 people) built out of logs. They usually had a wide doorways hung with buffalo hides, a number of window ports located on each side of the building, and hard-packed earthen floors. Wegiwas, in contrast, were built using foundation poles, which were tapered poles of wood that were somewhat flexible at their tops. The thicker, firmer ends of the poles were stuck in the ground in a circular, rectangular, or oval shape, while the thinner, more flexible ends were bent in and lashed together to form the frame for the roof. The structure was then covered with animal skins or tree bark, leaving a hole in the center of the roof to allow smoke from cooking and heating fires to escape. Animal skins were also used as floor coverings. Summer wegiwas had a rectangular or elongated oval floor plan and either a gabled or arched

Shawnee women make sugar from tree sap in this engraving. Most Shawnee women did not hunt; however, the food they gathered and cultivated formed a large and essential part of the tribe's diet.

roof, while winter wegiwas were smaller circular buildings with domed roofs. The Shawnees often moved at a moment's notice, so wegiwas were sparsely furnished, but unlike Native Americans further west, the Shawnees did not build portable houses, since building material was quite plentiful in the eastern woodlands and narrow forest trails made moving housing impractical.

During the warm season, the Shawnees were usually stationary, staying in their villages and farming. The Shawnees used the slash-and-burn technique to clear an area for crops, and Shawnee women and children planted and tended corn, beans, squash, and pumpkins, using digging sticks. Corn was the Shawnees' most important food source other than meat, and they cultivated a variety of breeds, preserving the best ears of corn for seed. In addition to the cultivated crops, the Shawnees gathered wild plants such as persimmons and wild grapes. Shawnees who lived in the East made syrup and sugar from the sugar maple each spring; those who lived further west substituted soft maple, box elder, or hickory sap to make sweets.

In the fall, everyone got ready for the winter's hunt, preparing weapons and performing the fall Bread Dance, a ceremony performed to ensure good hunting. When winter came, the Shawnees would abandon their villages and live in hunting camps. Able-bodied men would go out in parties for days, killing game and hanging what they could not carry

home out of the reach of wolves. After contact with the Europeans, Shawnee hunters primarily used rifles in the hunt, but more traditional weapons included the bow and arrow, the club, and a bola made of a four-foot-long, cone-shaped piece of wood that was thrown at the forefeet of a running animal, causing it to fall. Shawnee hunters were quite skilled at using animal calls to attract prey, a technique that backfired in one case when a hunter was seized by a panther who apparently thought he was another panther invading his territory; the big cat fled in terror when he discovered his mistake. Magic was used to improve hunting, and many men carried charms to lure game. Some hunters practiced a technique know as "medicine hunting," where they would sing magi-

Glass beads obtained from European traders were used by the Shawnees to make wampum belts and to decorate clothing and accessories. This colorful, men's beaded shoulder bag was made in the early or mid-19th century.

Metal was another item introduced to the Shawnees by the Europeans. The Shawnees quickly adopted metal weapons and cooking implements; they also formed a fondness for decorative metal jewelry, such as the engraved silver breastplate shown here.

cal songs and perform rituals to attract game to the camp. When the hunting party returned to camp, the hunters would rest overnight and then go back for the game left behind. The women and children skinned the game, prepared the skins and furs for use or trade, and sliced and preserved the meat by drying it on the roofs of the wegiwas. After hunting season passed, trapping season began, when hunters would catch smaller animals.

One of the many uses of the deer hides and buffalo skins gained from hunts was clothing. Shawnee dress was fairly subdued compared with that of neighboring tribes, although shirts were sometimes decorated with dyed porcupine quills, bright-colored feathers, and paints. Men usually wore a loose shirt and women a longer overblouse; in cold weather, leggings were added. Leather moccasins were worn as shoes, and hats were made of wildcat, raccoon, or beaver skins. Boys wore their hair in short bobs, men wore long, loose hair, and women and girls wore long braids. While women usually went bareheaded, warriors always wore one feather in their hair, and men also sometimes wore what was called a roach headdress, which consisted of fringes of long porcupine hair or turkey beards combined with shorter fringes of red deer hair sewn to a base in a shape that would stand erect on the wearer's head.

European traders brought metal items, and Shawnees of both sexes quickly formed a fondness for silver jewelry, wearing brooches, bracelets, medals, nose rings, and heavy earrings. (This plethora of silver among the Shawnees gave rise to rampant rumors of secret silver mines known only to the Shawnees; even today their former territory in the Ohio River valley is occasionally searched by treasure hunters.) A more ominous change in 18th-century Shawnee dress was the increasing number of garments and ornaments taken from European settlers who had fallen victim to Shawnee attacks—items that testified to the increasing violence of the struggle between the Shawnees and the settlers for land. Although their traditions had served the Shawnees well, the ever-growing population of white settlers and the mayhem they brought with them would soon fundamentally alter the Shawnee way of life. ▲

This page is from an account book that lists the various items traded between Native Americans and Europeans from 1645 to 1726. Several drawings of beavers appear in the upper right of the page. Although trade with the Europeans brought useful goods to the Shawnees, they quickly became dependent upon these goods and could no longer be self-reliant.

THIS

LAND

IS

OUR

LAND

By the mid-1700s, the French and British competition for land had reached a furious pace in and around the Ohio Valley and Great Lakes area. In early 1754, in an attempt to halt French expansion, the British began to build a fort at the confluence of the Monongahela and Allegheny rivers in western Pennsylvania. In April, French troops swooped in, captured the unfinished fort, completed its construction, and named it Fort Duquesne. A force of Virginians, led by a relatively unknown colonel named George Washington, marched to the fort to retake it as both sides recruited Indian allies to bolster their cause. The French commander, Captain Pierre de Contrecoeur, convinced the Delawares, Senecas, and the majority of the Shawnees to fight on the French side. The combined French and Indian troops quickly forced Washington's surrender at the Battle of Fort Necessity, marking the beginning of the conflict known as the French and Indian War.

In 1755, another British force, led by General Edward Braddock, marched on Fort Duquesne and was routed by French and Indian troops, with the Indians being led by an outstanding Shawnee Kishpoko war chief named Pucksinwah. The Shawnees then tried to woo their old enemies the Iroquois into the French alliance but were unsuccessful, and the Iroquois remained in the British camp. Despite the early French victories, the war turned in favor of the British, and in September 1758 the British retook Fort Duquesne, reinforcing it and renaming it Fort Pitt (the site of present-day Pittsburgh). The French quickly retreated from the area, followed by many of their Shawnee allies.

The decision of these Shawnees to fight on the side of the French was guided, as would be similar alliances, more by self-interest than by loyalty to either the British or the French. Unlike the British, the French in Shawnee territory were mostly traders, not land-hungry settlers, and the primary goal of the Shawnees was to keep their hunting grounds free of settlers while assuring themselves of a constant supply of trade goods, especially guns and ammunition. This goal would remain the motivating force behind Shawnee decisions to make war, sign treaties, or form alliances.

The British victory in the Ohio Valley area could have resulted in disastrous reprisals against the Shawnees, but thanks to their loose political organization, a number of Shawnee bands had allied themselves with the British and provided the redcoats with arms and ammunition. Consequently, these bands were allowed to stay in the Ohio River valley, and no doubt because of their cooperation with the British, some of the French-allied Shawnee bands were able to negotiate a truce with the British. Soon the Ohio River valley was again a major Shawnee population center.

French Quebec fell to the British in September 1759, and one year later, Montreal fell, effectively ending the French and Indian War in favor of the British. However, the end of the war did not mark the end of the influx of white settlers, and the Shawnees, along with the Delawares, Miamis, Ottawas, Cayugas, Senecas, Susquehannocks, and Wyandots, met with the British soon after the war to complain about the influx of new frontiersmen entering and settling on Indian land in Ohio and Kentucky. The tribes agreed to halt all raids against the new settlers, and the British promised to prohibit any whites except fur traders from entering these territories.

But settlement continued, and the British fur traders brought problems as well. By 1770, approximately 800,000 pounds of deerskins had been exported from the American colonies, and beaver, fox, mink, and otter pelt were also in demand. The whites traded guns and ammunition, horses, tools, utensils, and other material goods for the skins and furs. Although these goods improved Indian life, the Native Americans were becoming more and more dependent on them to survive, and their ability to provide for themselves was declining. As a result, Native Americans began locating their settlements closer to the major forts and trading posts.

In addition, there were noticeable differences between the ousted French colonial government and the newly installed British one. French traders had often freely dispensed trade goods and provisions to the Indians to win and hold their loyalty, but the British would only distribute these goods in exchange for furs, not realizing that many of these goods were now essential for the survival of the Native Americans. Due to the communal nature of tribal life, where

Native Americans and the commanders at Fort Pitt negotiate terms for releasing hostages after Pontiac's War. Although the allied Indian tribes were unsuccessful at driving the British out of the Ohio Valley, their attacks did gain them a number of concessions from the British colonial government.

resources were shared to ensure the survival of the tribe and to emphasize the bonds between allies, the reluctance of the British to share their wealth was viewed by the Native Americans as tantamount to a declaration of hostility. Additionally, the goal of the French colonial administration had been simple: maintain good relations with the Native Americans so the fur trade would thrive. In contrast, the British wanted to colonize the area in a more thorough and expansive way by developing other resources such as rivers and farmland, in addition to the fur trade.

The frustration of the Native Americans in the Ohio Valley mounted until a confederacy of Indian tribes (including the Shawnees) organized by an Ottawa chief named Pontiac rebelled against the British during the summer of 1763. The rebellion was, for a time, quite successful. One Shawnee war party, led by the principal chief of the Shawnee, Hokolesqua—more commonly known as Cornstalk—went as far as West Virginia, killing settlers and burning farms. Another party, led by Pucksinwah, attacked settlements and two forts in eastern Pennsylvania before laying a brief seige to Fort Pitt. Pontiac's War lasted until October, when the French, in response to Pontiac's repeated appeals for military aid, revealed that a treaty ending the French and Indian War had been signed with the British back in February and that a formal peace now existed between France and Britain.

Without the hope of French support, the Indians withdrew their troops, but their rebellion had jarred the British government into realizing the need for change. The British drew up the Royal Proclamation of 1763, reserving all lands west of the Alleghenies for the Indians and prohibiting Indian land purchases except by royal agents. In addition, a strict new licensing system was inaugurated, controlling who and what was traded to the Indians. This system was created in part because of repeated requests by Shawnee leaders—made as early as 1701—for the prohibition of whiskey in their territory. The trade controls, however, proved detrimental to the Native Americans, further restricting the availability of essential goods while proving ineffective in controlling the whiskey trade.

Despite the tensions, a tenuous peace prevailed between the British government and Native Americans until the signing of the Fort Stanwix Treaty in 1768. Fort Stanwix, located at the headwaters of the Mohawk River in New York, was the site of a meeting between representatives from New Jersey, New York, Virginia, and Pennsylvania, and the head of the Iroquois Confederation, along with approximately 3,000 Iroquois. The Iroquois, still hostile to the Shawnees, still claiming to be in charge of all other northeastern tribes, and still eager to give away other tribes' land, agreed in the treaty that the boundary line between white and Indian settlement should be moved from the Alleghenies to the Ohio River, opening the area that now encompasses Tennessee, Kentucky, and western Virginia to white

The Cumberland Gap, a low pass through the Cumberland Mountains at the junction of present-day Virginia, Kentucky, and Tennessee, was first discovered by British explorers in 1750. The pass formed a natural conduit for the wagons and horses of European settlers coming from the East and channeled the flow of pioneers directly into Shawnee territory.

settlement. In return, the whites paid £10,000 to the Iroquois, who were supposed to disperse it to the affected tribes but instead kept the money. The Fort Stanwix Treaty was a devastating blow to many tribes, but it was especially harmful to the Shawnee, as the Iroquois ceded their land claims directly to a land speculator representing the colonial governor of Virginia.

Once again the Shawnees had had their land sold out from under them by the Iroquois, and once again the sale had been accepted by the British, who undoubtedly knew that the treaty was a farce but accepted it in order to acquire land. This time, the Shawnees could not simply ignore the Iroquois's agreement; land surveyors, some of them hired by wealthy landowners in the East (including Patrick Henry and George Washington) immediately appeared in the Shawnee hunting grounds in Kentucky (the land nearest to the Cumberland Gap, which was a low pass through the Allegheny Mountains that could easily be crossed from the east), mapping the land so that it could be sold.

The Shawnees were enraged by the Fort Stanwix Treaty, but with the French gone and the failure of Pontiac's War, they lacked the European and Indian allies they needed to force change. They were already well established in the Ohio valley area, however, and they resolved to defend their territory. The behavior of the whites who arrived in that region only stiffened their resolve. White hunters repeatedly entered their hunting grounds and slaughtered needed animals for their furs or other mementos, leaving the meat to rot—a practice the Shawnees found shockingly wasteful. In addition, the majority of frontiersmen were extremely hostile to any and all Native Americans and would shoot them on sight without provocation, earning themselves the name "Indian haters." The Shawnees began to programmatically expel, harass, or execute any white surveyors or hunters they found on their lands.

In 1769, the Shawnees captured an exploring party led by Daniel Boone. The Indians made the whites take them to all their camps, where they destroyed or confiscated all the whites' property. The Shawnees then released the party unharmed, kindly supplying each member with a pair of moccasins, a gun, and a doeskin for patch leather, so that they would survive their trip home. The frontiersmen, however, were not impressed by the treatment they received; on the contrary, they were incensed at being kicked off land to which they believed the Shawnees had no valid claim.

The Shawnees were taking a good many white prisoners at this time, and despite their reputation for savagery, their treatment of prisoners varied a great deal depending on the captive's age and gender and the circumstances under which they were taken. Most commonly, prisoners of the Shawnees were either adopted by families that had lost a member or made to run a torture gauntlet or, sometimes, both. On June 5, 1771, 17-year-old Marmaduke van Swearingen was taken (apparently not

Boonesboro in September 1778, shortly before it was attacked by the Shawnees. Fortified outposts of this type, designed to protect settlers and traders, sprang up in increased numbers throughout the Shawnees' land during the latter half of the 18th century.

entirely unwillingly) near his family's estate in western Virginia by Pucksinwah and his warriors. He was brought back to a Shawnee village and forced to run between two facing parallel lines of stick- and club-wielding Shawnees, who beat him with their weapons the entire way. Van Swearingen ran the gauntlet with impressive fortitude and courage, but he was knocked unconscious in the process and took two weeks to recover. (The gauntlet could be quite brutal, but it was sometimes gentle and more like a form of hazing—one adoptive Shawnee recalled whacking a prisoner with a piece of pumpkin, to the great approbation of the rest of the tribe. Ordinarily nonwarriors—women, the elderly, and especially children—were beaten very lightly.)

When Van Swearingen revived, he learned that Pucksinwah planned to adopt him. This necessitated an adoption ritual, where he was stripped, and his entire body painted various colors. Pucksinwah recited an ancient Shawnee adoption chant over him, after which Van Swearingen was led to the waters of the Scioto River by women who dunked him and scrubbed all the paint off him (and, they claimed, all the white out of him). He was led back to the msika-melwi and dressed in a blouse and buckskin leggings. His face was carefully painted, and a metal disk with an eagle feather attached to it was put in his hair. The villagers filed in, and taking seats on the mats on the floor, lit and smoked pipes. Pucksinwah said words over his new son and gave him his new name— Wehyahpiherhrsehnwh, or Blue Jacket, after the blue hunting jacket he was wearing on the day he was captured.

From that moment on, Blue Jacket was considered a Shawnee and considered himself one as well, taking to his new life and family immediately. Under Pucksinwah's tutelage, he quickly learned the language and became a popular member of the tribe. He never left his adopted family, eventually becoming a chief of the Mekoche division. Although most adoptees of the Shawnees did not reach Blue Jacket's leadership position, many of them remained with the Shawnees even when given the opportunity to return to their respective families. Indeed, when in 1764 the British had demanded that the Shawnees return all their captives to their families, a number of prisoners hid from their would-be liberators, and others, once returned to their families, escaped and rejoined the Shawnee.

Although those fortunate enough to be adopted were treated well, other captives, especially enemy warriors, were put to slow and horrible deaths. The captives would usually be shaved and painted, then tied loosely to a post near slow-burning firewood where they were slashed, stoned, and dismembered both before and after the flames were lighted. The entire community would be involved during these ritual tortures, and women often took the lead as a way of releasing their anger and grief over the men they had lost. Although the ordeals were gruesome, they not only satisfied the desire for revenge but were seen by the Shawnees as an important aspect of their traditional heroic codes. According to these codes, if a man went through the torture bravely, his performance would be greatly rewarded in the next life. During the wars with the whites, however, the cruel rituals served more to entertain than to develop hero-

A Shawnee hunter prepares to kill a deer. The rapid influx of settlers into what is now the state of Kentucky destroyed the wildlife the Shawnees relied on for survival through overhunting and habitat destruction.

ism, and many captured nonwarriors suffered horrible deaths. Yet the Shawnees were not unanimous in their support of torture, and there are many stories of both male and female leaders (most famously Tecumseh) who felt pity for the victims and would stop the torture or end the victims' lives quickly.

So when Daniel Boone was taken prisoner again in 1778 by none other than Blue Jacket, he was extremely fortunate in becoming the Shawnee's most famous adoptee. He was adopted by Cornstalk's successor as primary chief, Chiungalla, or Black Fish, and stayed with the tribe for three months, but his sympathies always remained with the whites. When Boone discovered that the Shawnees were planning to attack Boonesboro, a station in Kentucky that had been founded by and named after him, he escaped and managed to get to Boonesboro in time to warn the inhabitants and help them defend their fort.

But Boone was a mere nuisance compared to Lord Dunmore, the colonial governor of Virginia, who announced in 1774 that he would issue grants for land on both sides of the Ohio River. Dunmore's action angered the fur traders in the Pittsburgh area, who questioned the governor's authority to make such grants. Virginian settlers, in turn, were suspicious of the Pennsylvanian fur traders, who they viewed as too sympathetic to the Native Americans, and were extremely hostile to the Native Americans, especially the Shawnees. Tensions reached a head when a band of Shawnees killed five of the six members of a

Virginian surveying crew, then told the sixth that Pennsylvanian fur trader George Croghan had encouraged them to kill all white settlers encroaching on their territory. Dr. John Connolly, Virginia's magistrate of western Pennsylvania, advised his supporters to take up arms, and a group of Shawnees acting as diplomats were promptly murdered by Virginians.

The Shawnees appealed to their former allies, the Miamis, the Wyandots, and the Ottawas, for aid, but these tribes, hoping to use the Shawnees as a buffer between themselves and the whites to the south and east, decided that the Shawnees' hunting grounds in Kentucky were too far from their territory to be worth losing men over. The Delawares were both threatened and bribed by the Iroquois and Indian agent Sir William Johnson to keep them from allying with the Shawnees. Yet, through a bizarre set of circumstances, the Shawnees found themselves allied with the Mingoes, originally Seneca and Cayuga tribesmen from the Iroquois Confederation who had settled in the Ohio region and had become disassociated with that nation. In 1774, a Mingo named Talgayeeta, more commonly known as Logan or John Logan, was away from his camp along the Ohio when a drunken party of Virginians went to his camp and killed 13 women and children, including his entire family. Logan was a former Cayuga who had married a Shawnee woman (who had died a few years before from a European disease). Because of his pacifist beliefs, he had

Logan returns home to discover his murdered family. The tragedy of his family's slaughter converted Logan from a noted pacifist and accommodationist to a staunch military ally of the Shawnees.

become an expatriate to his own tribe and a leader of the Mingoes, and he was well known and well respected on the frontier by both whites and Indians. The local white community expressed genuine horror at the killing of Logan's family, but no efforts were made to find and punish those responsible. With the help of some Mingo and Shawnee warriors, Logan began retaliatory killings of Virginian settlers.

The colonial government reacted much more decisively to these killings—Dunmore, who had been preparing to invade Shawnee territory for some time, deployed approximately 3,000 troops

Lord Dunmore, the colonial governor of Virginia, combined a rapacious desire for territory with an utter disregard for Native American life. An appointee of the British crown, Dunmore was ultimately ousted by Virginians during the American Revolution.

against the Indians in an action that became known as Lord Dunmore's War. Dunmore's troops were split into two divisions: one of approximately 1,000 men led out of Fort Union in western Virginia by Colonel Andrew Lewis, and one of approximately 2,000 men led out of Fort Pitt by Dunmore himself. The two divisions were to meet near the confluence of the Ohio and Hockhocking rivers and from there identify and attack Shawnee settlements.

Lewis's troops were 60 miles south of the meeting place when they camped at Point Pleasant, a sandy point where the Great Kanawha River flows into the Ohio. The Shawnee, led by Cornstalk and numbering approximately 700 men—among them Logan, Blue Jacket, Pucksinwah, and Pucksinwah's 16-year-old son, Cheesauka—decided to attack this smaller force before it met with Dunmore's troops, but a combination of bad luck and fog ruined what was to be a surprise attack at dawn. During the course of the bloody battle, Pucksinwah—who had predicted his own death—was killed, and the Shawnees retreated when they received intelligence that reinforcements for Lewis's troops were close at hand.

Although the battle at Point Pleasant had gone relatively well for the Native Americans, it was obvious that they would be vastly outnumbered by Dunmore's full army, and the few warriors who had been sent by allied tribes quickly deserted. This left a reduced force made up almost entirely of Shawnee warriors (plus Logan and about 20 other Mingoes), and Cornstalk decided that the Shawnees would have to sue for peace. He met with Dunmore and agreed to a truce, but no written records were made of the negotiation, and the two sides gave conflicting accounts of what had happened. Colonial officials maintained that Cornstalk had agreed to abide by the Fort Stanwix Treaty, but the Shawnees declared that their only agreement had been to stop fighting. In any case, it was obvious that the underlying reasons for the conflict had not been addressed, and the resulting peace was to be a fragile one. Indeed, a new threat to peace would soon arise from the whites' council houses in the East—the American Revolution. ▲

Patrick Henry, the first elected governor of Virginia, attempted to cultivate peaceful relations with the Shawnees. The fierce competition between settlers and Native Americans for resources, however, made war all but inevitable.

THE
REVOLUTION
AND
ITS
AFTERMATH

The impact of the War of Independence on the Shawnee, while serious, was for the most part indirect. Most of the actual fighting between British royal troops and American rebels took place along the Atlantic coast, far to the east of Shawnee territory, and government officials were too busy waging war to focus on encouraging expansion into Shawnee territory. But the unrest in the East and the desire to avoid military service resulted in a huge new wave of whites migrating west in the years 1775–76. Cornstalk journeyed to Kentucky in 1776 and was shocked to see how the infiltration of whites was changing the land. Although the Shawnees were officially neutral at this point, after his journey Cornstalk surreptitiously attempted to create an anti-American alliance with other tribes. Other Shawnees engaged in more direct action, and attacks on white settlers in Kentucky became common, especially after the British command at Detroit began to provide Shawnees with more trade goods and to offer a bounty on American scalps and prisoners.

On November 10, 1777, Cornstalk, along with his son and another Shawnee, went to Fort Randolph to try and discuss the situation with the Virginians. The commander of the fort imprisoned the three men, planning to hold them as hostages, but a mob, led by frontiersmen and including several soldiers, broke into the hostages' room and shot all three numerous times, beating and mutilating their bodies. The murder of Cornstalk greatly distressed the Tory Dunmore's replacement as governor of

Cornstalk, the Shawnee primary chief during both Pontiac's War and Lord Dunmore's War. Despised by most whites due to his leadership of the Shawnee military resistance, Cornstalk was killed by a mob while visiting Fort Randolph in Virginia.

Virginia, Patrick Henry. Realizing the Shawnees would quickly seek revenge, Henry issued a formal apology and offered a reward for the arrest of the mob leaders, but the murderers were never brought to justice. As Henry feared, the first act of the new Shawnee principal chief, Black Fish, was to raise the tomahawk against the American settlers. Soon the Shawnees were British allies.

The Shawnees and the Delawares attacked Fort Randolph in the spring of 1778, but they were unable to take it, as it had been strongly fortified in anticipation of just such a retaliation. Joined by the Wyandots, Mingoes, and Miamis, they made numerous raids against white settlers, killing hundreds and sparking a mass exodus from the Ohio Valley. In retaliation, the Americans sent an expedition out from Fort Pitt under General Edward Hand to destroy a reported depot on the Cuyahoga River that the British were using to supply the Native Americans. Hand, however, intimidated by the Shawnees' reputation as warriors, turned his men back without reaching the river or meeting the enemy. On their return, Hand's men came across a small Delaware hunting camp near Fort Pitt that, as the able-bodied men (and their weapons) were out with a hunting party, was completely defenseless. Hand ordered the camp attacked, and his men killed a small boy, two women, and an old man, and took two other women captive. Hand was forced to resign after his Squaw Campaign, as this expedition was derisively called, but the damage to the American cause had already been done. A number of key American officials in the west, disgusted at Hand's behavior, defected to the British side, and many of the more pacifist Old Northwest tribes, realizing that the Americans posed a very real military threat to them, allied themselves with the British.

Unfortunately, the threat of American military action proved too much for the relatively newfound Shawnee solidarity. In March 1779, a Thawikila chief, speaking in front of a Shawnee council, tomahawked in two a wampum belt that symbolized Shawnee unity, signaling a split within the Shawnee tribe. Many Shawnees were unhappy with the militancy of their current leadership and were afraid that antagonizing the Americans, who had superior numbers and weapons, would lead to disastrous reprisals. Most of the members of the Thawikila, Pekowi, and Kishpoko divisions (among them Pucksinwah's wife, Methotasa, who had been adopted after his death by the Pekowis) moved westward, settling in 1780 in what is now southeastern Missouri. Although the Shawnees had disbanded many times in both the recent and ancient past, this split was unique both in its size and in the type of disagreement that provoked it. The Shawnees who left—approximately 4,000 people—believed that retreating before the white settlers was the only means of ensuring their survival, while those who stayed—less than 3,000 people, including a mere 850 warriors—were equally certain that losing their territory to the whites would be worse than death.

The remaining Shawnees raised the tomahawk against the settlers with renewed fervor, if reduced numbers. The British surrender at Yorktown in

Militiamen slaughter the Moravian Delawares at Gnadenhutten. The viciousness of this massacre—in which 90 unarmed people, including 70 women and children, were killed—was excessive even for the time, and it enraged the Ohio Valley Indians.

1781 had little effect on the hostilities in the Ohio Valley, and atrocities rapidly accumulated on both sides. An incident that was extreme even by the bloody standards of the time was the massacre of the Moravian Delawares. The Moravians (a Protestant Christian sect) had sent missionaries to the Ohio Valley more than a decade before and had won over some converts, primarily Delawares. With these converts, the missionaries had established a commune at Gnadenhutten, on the Tuscarawas River, where by 1781 around 200 Native Americans farmed and raised cattle. The British and their Indian allies became concerned that the Moravians were supplying food and information to the Americans, so British officer Matthew Elliott and a party of Wyandots and Shawnees moved the entire commune from their farms in Gnadenhutten to a camp on the Sandusky River and took the missionaries to Detroit to be interrogated. After the missionaries returned to the camp, the half-starving commune was allowed to return to Gnadenhutten in the winter of 1782 to attempt to salvage their harvest.

Upon hearing of their return, a group of Americans, assuming that the Moravian Delawares were British agents (actually, there is some evidence that the missionaries were supplying information to the Americans), organized a company of militia to deal with these "hostile" Indians. The company went to Gnadenhutten, drove the converted Indians (some 20 men and 70 women and children) into a council house, and cold-bloodedly murdered the entire commune with hand weapons and tools. One man, Charles Builderback, personally brained 13 or 14 of the Moravian Delawares, then told a companion, "My arm fails me. Go on in the same way. I think I have done pretty well."

Although the Moravian Delawares had been distrusted by the British-allied tribes, the massacre infuriated the Native Americans, and they waited for a chance to take revenge. It came in the spring of 1782 when William Crawford, a friend of George Washington's and a successful businessman, raised a militia company to undertake what was proudly called the Second Moravian Campaign, an attack on the Indians before their summer raids began. Crawford led his 500 volunteers into a Delaware, Wyandot, and Shawnee ambush of approximately 1,000 warriors. The undisciplined militia immediately broke and ran, and 100 Americans were killed or captured, among them Crawford. Although Crawford had not been involved in the Gnadenhutten massacre, he was now commander of the militia, and the decision was made by the Delawares to make him pay for the crimes of his countrymen. Crawford was beaten with clubs, 70 rounds of black powder were fired into his naked body, and his ears were chopped off. He was then placed in a fire ring, and hot coals were thrown on his face and stomach. A friend of Crawford's was forced by the Delawares to watch the torture. The friend, who was supposed to be handed over to the Shawnees, managed to escape and return to the Americans with his grisly report. The fate of Crawford, a cultured Virginia gentleman, horrified the American public and emboldened Indian haters at all levels of society.

One year after Crawford's death, the Americans and the British signed the Treaty of Paris, officially ending the American Revolution. The treaty caused a great deal of distress and confusion among the Shawnees in the Ohio Valley, since the American officials informed them that the British had given up all lands west of the Appalachians and that Shawnee territory was now the property of the American government, while the British insisted that they had only given up political control of the western

The torture of captives, especially the use of the stake and the fire (which was built close enough to the captive to burn him but not close enough to kill him), was a common practice among both the Delawares and the Shawnees. Those who had or were believed to have had wronged the tribes in the past, such as the unfortunate William Crawford, suffered particularly brutal punishments.

regions and that the Shawnees' territory was still their own. By the terms of the treaty, the British surrendered to the Americans an enormous territory extending from the Great Lakes on the north to Spanish Florida on the south and the Mississippi on the west—a territory that obviously enclosed the Shawnees' land. The treaty terms, however, were nebulous as to the exact time when the British would give up the territory, and they were in no hurry to leave. The Americans may have had control on paper, but British troops still had actual possession of forts at Detroit, Niagara, and many other western locales of strategic importance.

In the face of this insecurity about their territory, a number of the Ohio Valley tribes met in 1783 to form a confederacy that advocated the continued acceptance by the American government of the 1768 Fort Stanwix Treaty, which had established the Ohio River as the boundary between Indian and American territory. The Americans refused to recognize the treaty, however, because it had been drawn up by the British colonial government. On account of the failure of the treaty to protect their territory, the Native Americans resorted to more violent tactics, attacking wagon trains and supply boats belonging to white settlers.

In January 1786, representatives of the United States met with a delegation of Shawnees, which they intimidated into signing a treaty that gave up the Shawnees' claims to lands east of the Miami River and acknowledged the sovereignty of the United States over all of their villages. In December 1786, another conference was called by the United States, but the Shawnee leaders refused to attend when they learned that the United States had no intention of giving up its extensive claims in Ohio. Finally, a few accommodationist members of the Wyandot, Delaware, and Seneca tribes met with the U.S. authorities and agreed to validate the United States' claims in eastern Ohio. The Shawnees, however, continued to refuse to recognize these claims.

The government's response to Shawnee resistance was initially fairly weak. During the year 1789 alone, 20,000 new settlers had entered the Ohio Valley, but they were not considered particularly loyal to the new American government. Most of them had headed west because of a dislike for the social or economic conditions in the East and were considered misfits or worse by the federal government. The first secretary of war, Henry Knox, referred to the western settlers as "lawless adventurers," and in some government circles they were considered to be as much of a problem as the Native Americans. Consequently, the repeated calls from the settlers for some sort of military solution to their various conflicts with northwest tribes were repeatedly turned down in favor of the cheaper approach of manipulating and intimidating tribal chiefs into signing away land.

By the late 1780s, however, the economic situation in the United States had deteriorated, and politicians began to

The new American government proved far more aggressive about appropriating Indian territory than the British. Soon settlers were clearing extensive new stretches of land, destroying the woodlands the Native Americans needed to survive.

look to the "unsettled" western territory as a potential money-maker. In 1787, Congress passed the Northwest Ordinance, which federalized most of the country west of the Alleghenies, north of the Ohio, and east of the Mississippi—an area including present-day Ohio, Indiana, Michigan, Illinois, Wisconsin, and eastern Minnesota. This vast territory was not divided into states; instead, Congress assigned a federal governor, Arthur St. Clair, who was authorized to establish and maintain law and to oversee the sale of public lands. The settlers—and the land speculators—were overjoyed.

To firmly establish U.S. rule over the Northwest Territory (later called the Old Northwest), President George Washington created a federal army of 1,216 men in 1790, most of whom were promptly sent out west. This movement of troops alarmed not only the Shawnees but also the British forces occupying Detroit. St. Clair, eager to avoid starting a war with the British, wrote the commander of Fort Detroit, explaining that his troops would be kept strictly to anti-Indian expeditions and that the current expedition had as its target the Shawnee village of Kekionga. The British at Detroit, taking advantage of St. Clair's naïveté, passed on his informative letter to the Shawnees and quietly reinstated their Revolution-era policy of offering Native Americans $50 for each American scalp and $100 for each live prisoner. Meanwhile, the hapless leader of the Kekionga attack, General Josiah Harmar, raised 1,500 militiamen—mostly settlers with no pre-

vious military experience—from Kentucky and Pennsylvania and set off. Under the command of Blue Jacket, the Shawnees and their allies the Miamis ambushed a detachment of Harmar's forces and soundly defeated them. Harmar immediately ordered a retreat.

The defeat of Harmar instilled great confidence in the Shawnee forces, but no military victory could disguise the hardship the Shawnees suffered that winter. Harmar's men had managed to destroy Shawnee food reserves before they were attacked, and earlier attacks by American forces had destroyed a number of Shawnee villages, including their largest village, Chalahgawtha. The Shawnees survived the winter by raiding settlers' farms and boats for supplies, and the Americans retaliated by offering $50 per Indian scalp. Hostilities between the Shawnees and the Americans increased until the possibility of the United States launching a full-scale attack against the northwest tribes was raised in several diplomatic circles.

To stave off such an attack, which might spill over into Canada, Britain sent representatives to both the Americans and the northwest Indians, offering to act as intermediaries in the establishment of a treaty. The British suggested giving the Indians in perpetuity all the lands north of the Ohio River and west of the Muskingum River—creating, in essence, a permanent, neutral buffer zone between the United States and Canada. Both parties rejected the offer.

Instead, Washington appointed St. Clair as leader of a new, larger military

General Josiah Harmar led 1,500 militiamen in an attack against the Shawnees that quickly ended in retreat after a detachment of his forces were ambushed by warriors. Although his campaign was a military failure, his troops destroyed Shawnee crops and food supplies, creating massive hardship that winter.

force. A Revolutionary War veteran, St. Clair was by this time well past his prime and was obese and gout-ridden. The men who volunteered for service were once again new to war, and St. Clair fell over 1,000 troops short of his goal of 2,500. The expedition left Fort Hamilton in southwestern Ohio on October 4, 1791, and was immediately plagued with problems. The men had to cut roads through the forest, which exhausted them before any fight had begun; the food was of terrible quality and insufficient quantity, thanks to dishonest quartermasters; the men's boots, issued by the government, quickly fell apart; and the army had an entourage of 200 camp followers—mostly officers' families and prostitutes—who severely hampered the troops' mobility. The wet, hungry, tired soldiers began to desert by the hundreds.

On top of everything else, St. Clair's forces were being spied upon. Scouts were reporting all the hardships suffered by the Americans to the Indian war chiefs, who wisely decided to hold off their attack for a few weeks and allow the Americans to exhaust themselves. Finally, on November 3, St. Clair's army, reduced by desertion and the manning of hastily constructed forts to less than 1,000 men, camped at the headwaters of the Wabash River without building any protective fortification to defend themselves—precisely the sort of mistake the Native Americans were waiting for. Early the next morning, as St. Clair's men were preparing their weapons and equipment, they were attacked by a large force of Shawnee, Miami, Potawatomi, and Delaware warriors, led once again by Blue Jacket. St. Clair's conduct throughout the battle was commendable—despite being crippled by a severe attack of gout, he managed to stay in the thick of the fighting and direct his men, and although eight bullet holes were later found in his hat and clothing, he escaped unhurt. But his courage was wasted; his undisciplined troops were immediately thrown into disarray by the attack, and what began as a battle ended as a massacre. After three hours, over 600 men were killed, over 250 were severely wounded, and the entire entourage of camp followers was slaughtered. While estimates of Native American casualties vary, probably less than 100 were killed or wounded. St. Clair's defeat remains the greatest Indian military victory over an American force in history.

Washington was enraged by the defeat, and considered the United States to now be at war with the northwest Indians. Curiously enough, Washington's view was in opposition to that of the majority of eastern Americans, who were, for the first time in American history, inclined to make peace with the Native Americans in the west. As a result, when Congress finally granted Washington funds to raise an army of 5,000 men to march against the Shawnees and their allies, it was under the condition that Washington first make a major effort to arrange a peace treaty.

Members of Washington's cabinet, including Henry Knox, Alexander Hamilton, and Thomas Jefferson, informed

Arthur St. Clair, the federal governor of the Northwest Territory, led his undisciplined and ill-supplied troops into the greatest military defeat ever suffered by U.S. forces at the hands of the Native Americans. St. Clair miraculously survived his troop's massacre without serious injury; after the battle, eight bullet holes were found in his hat and clothing.

the British that they were now interested in the British offer to act as intermediaries in setting up a peace treaty. The British, still wanting to create an Indian buffer zone between the United States and Canada, sent six messengers into the Northwest Territory. Unfortunately, after St. Clair's defeat, the Native Americans were confident they could forcibly keep the whites out, and all six were killed.

Finally, an Iroquois delegation agreed to enter Shawnee territory, and the Shawnees, although expressing distrust for both the Iroquois and the Americans, agreed to meet with them. The American terms for peace established a boundary line along the Muskingum River, leaving everything west and north of the Ohio for the Indians, except what had already been settled by whites. The Shawnees, led by Blue Jacket, rejected this offer and stipulated that any truce must give the Native Americans complete control of all the land north of the Ohio, and any white settlers in that area would have to leave. In addition, the Shawnees wished to be reimbursed for their Kentucky hunting grounds, which had been ruined by white settlement. The Iroquois delegation realized that the Americans would never accept the Shawnees' terms, so upon their return, they simply altered the Shawnees' reply to suit their American audience. All the parties agreed to meet again the following year.

In the meantime, Washington began the search for a new commander for the 5,000 regulars who were to be led into the heart of hostile Indian territory. Anthony Wayne, another obese, gouty man of questionable reputation, was selected. Wayne had performed well in the Revolutionary War, being promoted to brigadier general, but his two nicknames—Dandy Tony and Mad Anthony—testified to his heavy drinking, his womanizing, his extreme vanity, and his irritability. Wayne, however, was aware of his mixed reputation and was determined to prove himself by succeeding where others had failed. Once his troops reached their fort on the Ohio River, Wayne, ever the disciplinarian, put months into training them, and he was the first western commander to study the history, culture, and military tactics of the western Indians. The only thing that stood in Wayne's way, once he felt his troops were ready, was public opinion—as Henry Knox wrote him, "The sentiments of the great mass of Citizens of the United States are adverse in the extreme to an Indian War."

The following year, American representatives attended a council of 16 western Indian tribes—or rather, their British and Iroquois intermediaries attended, as the Americans did not dare appear in person. The Shawnees immediately demanded to know the purpose of the large American army now gathered on the Ohio River, and the intermediaries replied that it was solely a defensive force. The Americans, continued the intermediaries, admitted that they had been wrong in thinking that because they had defeated the British in the American Revolution, they had also

(continued on page 73)

RECORDING TRADITIONAL LIFE

The success of the Shawnees in retaining their ancestral ways is recorded in the watercolor paintings of Shawnee artist Earnest Spybuck. Born an Absentee Shawnee of the Thawikila division in Oklahoma in 1883, Spybuck began drawing at an early age. He later maintained that "Mother Earth started me drawing." Though his limited formal education did not include any art training, his talent brought him to the attention of anthropologist Mark Raymond Harrington. Upon seeing Spybuck's paintings, Harrington offered to pay him to record scenes of traditional Shawnee home and ceremonial life. Between 1910 and 1921, Spybuck produced 27 watercolor paintings for Harrington, detailing aspects of Shawnee life and that of tribes on neighboring reservations. Some of those paintings are reproduced on these pages. Spybuck, who eventually became a leader of the Peyote religion, continued painting until his death in 1949.

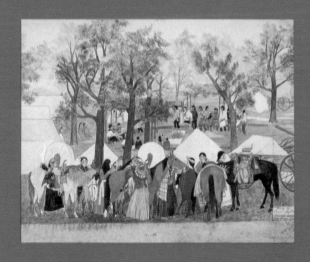

Shawnee Indians Having Cornbread Dance (ca. 1910)

In Spybuck's time, the Bread Dance ceremony consisted of a three-day hunt by the men, followed by a feast prepared by the women. In this picture, the men have just returned from hunting and can be seen dancing in the background, while the women remove the resulting game from their horses.

Shawnee Home About 1890 (ca. 1910)

This painting recreates a scene from Spybuck's boyhood on the Absentee Shawnee Reservation in Oklahoma. Two hunters return with game while three women prepare food with a mix of traditional and manufactured utensils.

67

Sauk and Fox Drum Dance (ca. 1910)

By Ernest L. Spybuck
7644

Spybuck traveled to neighboring
tribes to record their ceremonies
as well as those of the Shawnees.
This painting depicts a Sac and Fox
religious ceremony called the Drum
Dance or the Dream Dance. The white
flags with red crosses on them are the
symbol of a Sac and Fox society called
the Midewiwin Society.

Sauk and Fox Emerging from Sweat House During Midewiwin Ceremony (ca. 1910)

Women rinse off members of
the Midewiwin Society as they
emerge from a sweat-lodge ritual
held in the large, central tent.

Moccasin Game (ca. 1910)

A group of Shawnees play a shell game in which one player, using sleight of hand, hides an object under one of three moccasins and the other players try to guess which moccasin contains the object. The man hiding the object (wearing a blue shirt and a feather in his hair in this painting) must move it and the moccasins in time with a song he is singing; the other players smoke and keep time. The red and white folded blankets are probably the wager in the game.

(continued from page 64)

defeated the western Indians and had obtained title to their lands by right of conquest. Because the United States recognized this error in its thinking, it agreed to withdraw all claims to land north of the Ohio River except for certain areas around the Cincinnati, Scioto, and Muskingum rivers, which contained white settlements. In addition, the United States would agree to pay the lump sum of $50,000 and an annuity of $10,000 as reparations to the nations that lost those areas.

After two weeks of deliberation, the 16 tribes sent back their response. They demanded once again that all territory north of the Ohio River be recognized as indubitably theirs, free from any white settlements. They rejected the offer of reparations, suggesting that the money

General Anthony Wayne leads his troops in a charge at Fallen Timbers, Ohio. Wayne proved a vigorous commander, threatening to shoot his men if they deserted, and his forces quickly defeated the smaller Native American army.

earmarked for that purpose be given to the white settlers in Native American territory so that they could afford to move out. Certainly, the response concluded, the United States could afford to pay off all those settlers, especially if they considered the expense necessary to raise an army against the tribes. The United States government, which had been fairly cool to the idea of peace with the Native Americans all along, decided that there was no point in continuing the talks. The Washington administration quickly convinced Congress that serious peace overtures had been made and rejected.

Wayne spent almost a full year after the breakdown of the talks preparing for war, drilling and hardening his men. His patience not only improved his own force but weakened the Native American coalition of tribes as well, since warriors from allied tribes who were expecting an attack soon after the failed negotiations eventually became bored and returned to their villages. Finally, in the fall of 1794, Wayne began to march his army of over 3,500 men westward, destroying the Shawnee crops and villages in their path. The extensive training paid off; Wayne's men were well-disciplined and his army speedy, and as they progressed, they threw up a large number of forts, firmly establishing an American military presence in the area. The Native American army at this time consisted of 1,500 Ottawa, Potawatomi, Miami, Delaware, Wyandot, and Shawnee warriors, led by Blue Jacket. Although outnumbered, they hoped to

Wayne listens to a speech during the negotiations for the Treaty of Greenville. The treaty resulted in the surrender of hundreds of thousands of acres of Native American land north of the Ohio River, much of it Shawnee territory.

ambush Wayne's men, a strategy that had proved effective in similar situations. In addition, the Native Americans had been promised aid by the British, and they had 70 white Canadian militiamen (disguised as Indians to conceal Britain's role in the hostilities) in their force.

The war party readied themselves for battle at a spot in present-day Ohio later known as Fallen Timbers. A forested area that had been hit by a tornado some years before, Fallen Timbers provided perfect cover for the Native Americans—and it was near the British Fort Miamis, where the warriors were certain they could take shelter if forced to retreat. With Wayne's troops nearby, the warriors began a fast, which was the traditional preparation for a battle. Wayne was aware of this tradition, however, and to weaken his enemy, waited an additional two days before moving. Moreover, a cold rain fell the night before the battle, chilling the Native Americans, who slept in the open air, but not affecting Wayne's tented troops. Finally, on August 20, 1794, the Americans charged Fallen Timbers.

The battle went poorly for the Native Americans, who for once formed the less disciplined army. The Ottawa contingent moved too quickly, cutting a large hole in the Indian formation line and ruining any possibility of surprise. When the American troops showed signs of panic, Wayne galloped into the battle and offered to shoot any deserters. With this motivation, the Americans began a determined offensive against the Indians, who began to lose ground quickly. Within an hour, Blue Jacket ordered a retreat to Fort Miamis.

Casualties had been fairly light in the Battle of Fallen Timbers, so it was a large party of chiefs and warriors who fled to the fort—only to discover the gates barred against them. Fearful of American reprisals, the commander of Fort Miamis informed the Native Americans pounding on the gates that the British would shoot anyone who tried to climb the palisades. Betrayed by their British allies, the Native Americans scattered into the woods, as Wayne's forces rapidly approached the fort. Fortunately for the Native Americans, Wayne halted the pursuit in favor of taunting the fortressed British troops. Wayne's army then continued down the Maumee River, destroying every Indian village or crop in sight, as Blue Jacket and the other Shawnees, bedraggled and defeated, hid out in camps on Lake Erie, well into British territory.

In winter of 1795, Blue Jacket and his followers visited Wayne's headquarters in Greenville, Ohio, to sue for peace. Other chiefs did the same, and in the spring, 1,100 chiefs and warriors attended a treaty conference in Greenville, where they learned that the British, unwilling to risk war over the increasingly unprofitable Ohio Valley fur trade, had agreed to evacuate the Northwest Territory and retire to Ontario. The dominant power in the Northwest Territory was now undeniably the United States, and the fate of the northwest tribes seemed to rest in the Americans' hands.

The chiefs had no choice but to agree to a punitive peace treaty drawn up by Wayne.

Wayne's Treaty of Greenville created a firm boundary between the Indian territory and the area open to white settlement, but it demanded large land concessions, the largest being in Shawnee territory. It also stipulated that the United States be allowed to build and occupy forts in the newly designated Indian territory. In return, the United States promised to try to keep its citizens out of Indian territory and to better control unscrupulous traders, and the Native Americans were to receive a one-time payment of $20,000 (a $25,000 settlement minus $5,000 for the expense of the treaty council) and $9,500 each year thereafter, to be divided among the nations represented. In addition, the Americans offered Blue Jacket an honorary commission in the United States Army and a $300 annual annuity, which he accepted, effectively ending his career as a leader of armed resistance against the Americans.

Ninety-one chiefs representing 12 nations of the Ohio Valley and lower Great Lakes region signed the Treaty of Greenville in August 1795. But there was a notable absence. A certain 27-year-old Shawnee war chief named Tecumseh, renowned for his prowess and intelligence, had flatly refused to attend the conference or to sign any treaty with the whites. His absence was viewed as an act of admirable courage by the Indians and as an act of subversive defiance by the Americans. Tecumseh would prove both views correct. ▲

TECUMSEH.

The Shawnee warrior Tecumseh organized a militant multitribe alliance to resist American expansionism. Charismatic and astute, Tecumseh excelled both in military strategy and in eloquently elucidating the threat white settlers posed to the Native Americans.

5

TECUMSEH
AND
TENSKWATAWA

The warrior who showed such independence at Greenville came from a family of equally bold and forceful men. Tecumseh was the second son of Pucksinwah, the Shawnee warrior who was killed at the Battle of Point Pleasant. In his dying breaths, Pucksinwah had commanded his eldest son, Cheesauka, to train the six-year-old Tecumseh as a warrior and to never make peace with the whites. Cheesauka was as good as his word and excelled as both a warrior and a teacher, becoming quite close to his younger brother, and after their mother moved to Missouri in 1779, acting as a surrogate parent as well. By all accounts, Tecumseh was a model child, and although it is claimed that he ran in terror from his first battle, his courage never faltered from then on. Tall, muscu-

lar, intelligent, and highly charismatic, Tecumseh proved to be a master tactician and an exceptional orator.

When Tecumseh was in his twenties, he and Cheesauka made a number of lengthy expeditions, visiting other tribes and viewing the territory to the north and west of the Shawnees'. These voyages, considered a final rite of passage into the adult world by the Shawnees, introduced Tecumseh to other tribes and other traditions, no doubt contributing to his later pan-Indian thinking. One evening during their final journey together, Cheesauka serenely predicted his own death the next day. That noon, he was fatally shot while storming a fort with a Cherokee war party. Tecumseh returned from this sad trip in 1790 and joined up with his adoptive brother Blue

Jacket in the fight to preserve Shawnee territory from the white settlers. In battle, Tecumseh demonstrated his strength, skill, and leadership ability, while in council, he demonstrated his firm opposition to any concessions to the whites. He soon developed a circle of equally militant followers, including his younger brother, Tenskwatawa.

Tenskwatawa was one of a set of triplets born a few years after Tecumseh. One triplet, Sauwaseekau, was killed at the Battle of Fallen Timbers; the second, Kumskaka, may have died young, for there are no records of his life; and the third, who would eventually be known as Tenskwatawa, was a fussy baby who was given the name Lalawethika—He Makes a Loud Noise. Unlike Tecumseh, Lalawethika was a clumsy child who was woefully unskilled in hunting and would never become a warrior—a serious social handicap for a young man in Shawnee society. Lalawethika lost his right eye in an early hunting accident and, as he grew older, developed a fondness for whiskey that quickly degenerated into severe alcoholism. Despite his flaws, Lalawethika was devoted to Tecumseh, and the older brother acted as his protector.

Tecumseh's boycott of the treaty conference at Greenville resulted in a serious break with Black Fish's replacement as the principal chief of the Shawnees, Catahecassa, or Black Hoof. Tecumseh and his followers went to Deer Creek in western Ohio and in 1795 founded a village made up of Native American warriors linked by their militancy, not by their tribal affiliation.

Although Tecumseh is generally revered by Shawnees today, many of his followers were not Shawnees, and many Shawnees of the time viewed him as a troublemaker and an usurper of tribal authority. Tecumseh's unique achievements sometimes blind students of Shawnee history to the fact that at this time there were three main groups of Shawnees: the Shawnees in Missouri, the Shawnees under Black Hoof in Ohio, and the relatively small group of Shawnees that followed Tecumseh. These three groups used very different strategies in coping with the Americans at this time. The Shawnees in Missouri were now discovering white surveyors and frontiersmen—the advance guard of white settlement—in their lands, but the situation had not yet reached a crisis.

The Shawnees under Black Hoof cooperated with the U.S. government and attempted to assimilate into American society. Upon being told by Wayne that they could resettle their old villages provided they remain peaceful, Black Hoof's Shawnees reestablished the town of Wapakoneta, on the Auglaize River in western Ohio. Black Hoof visited Washington, D. C., in the winter of 1802–03, and asked Secretary of War Henry Dearborn for agricultural implements and training, and for legal title to the land inhabited by his Shawnees. Dearborn was much more inclined to grant the former than the latter, and he initiated efforts to establish a model farm and a Quaker mission on the Auglaize. William Kirk, an energetic missionary,

Black Hoof, leader of the Shawnees living in Wapakoneta, Ohio. Although it was fairly common in Shawnee tradition for a young warrior to start a new village if he disagreed with the current chief, Tecumseh's split with Black Hoof was not an amicable one, in part because Black Hoof feared that Tecumseh's militancy could bring reprisals on his village as well.

This sketch shows the first Methodist mission and school established among the Shawnees, which was founded in 1830.

was sent to Wapakoneta in 1807, where he immediately established an agricultural program, purchased breeder stock, began construction of a sawmill, and planned a grain mill. Unfortunately, Kirk failed to file the proper reports with the U.S. government; as a result, he was charged with not adequately accounting for federal funds, and his position was terminated in 1808. Without the necessary agricultural training, the Shawnees' fields fell into ruins, and most of Black Hoof's band became dependent upon the annuities handed out by the U.S. government.

Black Hoof's pro-American stance and the dependence of his people on annuities meant that Tecumseh's village received no supplies from the U.S. government, and thanks to the overhunting and habitat destruction that accompanied white settlers, living off the land became increasingly difficult. His village was forced to move from Deer Creek to the upper Miami Valley in 1796, then to an area along the Whitewater River in eastern Indiana in 1797, the year John Adams replaced George Washington as president of the United States. In 1800, Tecumseh and his band of approximately 100 followers moved again to live near some Delaware villages in east-central Indiana.

In 1801, Thomas Jefferson was elected president. An agrarian idealist, Jefferson envisioned the United States as a nation of "yeoman farmers"—landowning, independent people who lived off the land in the European sense of the phrase. It would be easier and better, he felt, to compel the Native Americans to conform with this ideal rather than to make the large land concessions necessary if they were to continue with their traditional hunter-and-gatherer lifestyle. In this effort, Jefferson found an invaluable ally in the new governor of the Indiana Territory, an ambitious young former aide of Wayne's (and future American president) named William Henry Harrison.

Jefferson, not wanting to raise any protest among Americans along the eastern seaboard (who had sympathetic, albeit hopelessly romanticized, notions of the western Indians), sent Harrison a confidential memo outlining his plan to convert the Native Americans to an agrarian way of life, and in the process, open up Indian land for white settlement. Harrison could force change in a bloodless way, Jefferson felt, by increasing the number of trading posts, enticing the Indians into going into debt (which, thanks to their limited incomes, they would be inclined to do), and then forcing them to sell their land (which, thanks

to their taking up European farming methods, they would not need) to pay their bills. Harrison and Jefferson both thought that if the Native Americans could only be made to live like whites, they would be much less of a headache for the United States.

Obviously, Jefferson's plan did not take into consideration the needs and desires of the Native Americans. Many were strongly loyal to their traditions and believed that living as whites was a fate worse than death. Others, such as Black Hoof's Shawnees, attempted to become a part of white American culture but found acculturation extremely difficult, and the short-lived and ineffective pilot project established at Wapakoneta was the rule rather than the exception as far as agricultural or business training for Native Americans was concerned. Jefferson had also not taken into consideration how much racial prejudice existed in the West, where Indian haters abounded and whites often violently competed with Native Americans for resources. Finally, Harrison had his own bloodless method of gaining Indian land, namely through highly dubious land purchases. Harrison became rather notorious among Native Americans for purchasing land (often with the help of bribes and intoxicants) from people with no right to sell it, such as minor chiefs without the authority to make decisions for an entire tribe or tribes that did not actually live on the purchased land, then zealously condemning those who opposed the purchases as lawless.

Things were looking fairly grim for the Native Americans in general at this time, but for at least one Native American, Lalawethika, things were positively dismal. His drinking had gone completely out of control, much to the detriment of his wife and children, and his incompetence in hunting (friends and relations had to provide his family with meat) led to his being an outcast in Tecumseh's warrior-dominated village. The one positive note in his life was his meeting a well-respected prophet and medicine man named Penagashea, who befriended him and shared with him some of his medical and magical knowledge, but Penagashea died in 1804 before Lalawethika's training was complete, and his subsequent attempts to perform healings were not successful.

In 1805, Lalawethika fell into a coma and appeared to stop breathing. His relatives were busy making funeral arrangements when, to their amazement, he stirred and came to his senses. He told them that he had in fact died and had been escorted into the spirit world, where he was shown the past and the future, heaven and hell, and most intriguingly, the way to defeat the white man. He renounced his evil ways, swore never to drink again, changed his name to Tenskwatawa (The Open Door) to go with his new persona, and set out to tell his people of his revelation.

Tenskwatawa, soon known simply as the Prophet, began to preach a doctrine of strict Native American unity, a unity that superceded tribal loyalties. Demanding that Native Americans return to their ancestral ways, he forbade his followers to consume or use anything that had been brought to North America by the whites, including alcohol, clothing made of woven fabric, metal tools, and the meat of domesticated livestock—but excluding firearms. Tenskwatawa's preaching appealed to many Native Americans in the Northwest, who were undergoing tremendous stress and hardship as a direct result of white encroachment. Military and legal means against the whites had failed them, and assimilation was unacceptable. Tenskwatawa offered a new, more spiritual solution that both addressed contemporary issues and was in keeping with traditional ways.

By this time, Tecumseh had begun to make a name for himself among the whites as well as the Native Americans as a pragmatic, eloquent, and intelligent leader. His practical leadership soon became necessary as followers of Tenskwatawa flocked to his village (which moved again in 1805 to an area just outside the now-abandoned Fort Greenville). While Tenskwatawa was instigating a spiritual revival, Tecumseh began to instigate a political movement that was no less revolutionary. The basis of Tecumseh's political philosophy was a recognition of the dire threat the whites posed to all Native Americans. He believed that no treaty or border or land agreement would successfully protect the land and the native peoples against the consuming greed of the whites. The

Tenskwatawa, also known as the Prophet, was a mystic visionary who envisioned a world purged of the baneful influence of the whites.

only way to combat this threat was for all the Indian tribes to unite—not in a loose, temporary confederation with each tribe under their own governance as was the norm, but in a single political body with a unified leadership. This way, if the whites wanted to purchase land or draw up a treaty, they would not be able to play one tribe off the other as they had in the past but instead would have to deal with a political body that represented the interests of all the tribes. If the whites wished to make war, they would have to face an enormous army comprising all the warriors of all the Indian tribes. This, felt Tecumseh, was the only way for the Native Americans to successfully protect what land and resources they still had.

The combination of the two brothers, one a political activist and the other a religious zealot, was powerful, and the size of their following grew. Tecumseh began to visit various tribes throughout the Northwest, filling the ears of all who cared to listen about the danger the whites posed to their land. Tecumseh was realistic about the Native Americans' chances of reclaiming land in the East, but he hoped to stop white expansion at the border agreed to in the Greenville Treaty. Despite Harrison's recent land purchases in Indiana, Illinois, Michigan, and Wisconsin, Tecumseh pointed out the questionable nature of such transactions and dismissed the United States' claims.

Tenskwatawa traveled as well, although not as extensively, going to Black Hoof's village on the Auglaize River and preaching several sermons where he made a number of converts. The Delawares, hearing of Tenskwatawa's condemnation of rival religious leaders and Indians who followed white ways as witches, invited him to come to their villages on the White River and help them purify themselves. One old woman accused of witchcraft was roasted over a slow fire for four days, and four others were tortured and put to death. Tenskwatawa moved on to some Wyandot villages on the Sandusky River, where more witches were found, but fortunately for them, their chief forbade their persecution. (Unlike Tenskwatawa, Tecumseh was always adamantly opposed to any use of torture.)

Harrison quickly learned of Tecumseh's travels to various tribes, but as he had not yet learned the nature of Tecumseh's visits, he was not unduly alarmed. When he heard of Tenskwatawa's witch trials, however, he sent a message to the Delawares, reprimanding them for listening to what Harrison maintained was a false prophet. Eager to expose Tenskwatawa as a fraud, Harrison advised the Delawares to demand some sign of divinity from the new prophet, adding, "If he is really a prophet, ask of him to cause to sun to stand still—the moon to alter its course—the rivers to cease to flow—or the dead to rise from their graves."

Harrison's strategy backfired when Tenskwatawa accepted the challenge, announcing that he would cause the sun to stand still on June 16, 1806, at Greenville. A large crowd showed up at the appointed place and time and observed a miracle—a dramatic total solar eclipse. The Americans protested that Tenskwatawa had somehow learned from some whites or an almanac when an eclipse was to take place, but many of the Indians who had been wavering were now convinced that he did have incredible supernatural powers. Pilgrims began to swarm to Tenskwatawa and Tecumseh's village as stories circulated that the Prophet could heal wounds and diseases and perform many other miraculous feats.

Although most of the visitors came to see Tenskwatawa, Tecumseh was able to further his political agenda, selecting his main lieutenants from among the pilgrims. While Tenskwatawa remained occupied by his religious activities, Tecumseh began to organize the community and to capitalize on the flow of people. Many pilgrims were converted to both Tenskwatawa's religion and Tecumseh's politics and preached both these messages when they returned to their own tribes.

Tecumseh's success was a cause of concern for the U.S. government, as a main objective of the Americans from the beginning of their struggle with the Indians had been to keep them divided. In April 1807, a messenger was sent to Tecumseh from a low-ranking federal agent warning him that he and his followers needed to vacate Greenville immediately, as they had settled there in violation of the Fort Greenville Treaty. Tecumseh informed the messenger that

if the president of the United States wanted to negotiate with him, he had better send someone of higher rank. The agent sent numerous messages to Harrison expressing his suspicions of the two brothers, but Harrison did not agree that they were a threat. He had demanded explanations of the brothers' activities in the past, but both had managed to convince him that they were simply pious, clean-living, politically neutral religious leaders. Harrison had even complimented Tecumseh in a letter written to the secretary of war, stating that he seemed to be a "bold, active, sensible man daring in the extreme and capable of any undertaking."

This tenuous goodwill was not to last. On June 22, 1807, far away on the Virginia coast, a British ship fired on an American frigate, an act that would eventually lead to the War of 1812. Americans were outraged at the British aggression, and many politicians, including Harrison, began to believe that war against Britain was inevitable. They also began to fear that the Native American tribes that had allied with the British during the Revolutionary War would do so again. In this atmosphere, Harrison could not help but notice the large, bustling, intertribal community outside of Greenville, which was attracting an alarming number of young, militant warriors from many different tribes. Soon American spies joined the pilgrims at Greenville.

Suspicions heightened when, in the spring of 1807, a number of settlers were killed by Native Americans in the

Tecumseh and William Henry Harrison engage in one of their more acrimonious debates concerning the legitimacy of Harrison's land purchases. While Tecumseh strongly believed that the United States should not be given any more Native American territory, Harrison just as fervently believed that it was the destiny of the United States to expand from ocean to ocean.

woods. Tecumseh and some of his men went to a conference in Springfield, Ohio, called by the whites to determine who was responsible for the killings. Black Hoof was also in attendance, and hostility between the two Shawnee leaders became evident as they blamed each other for instigating the attack. Black Hoof claimed the Tecumseh was a dangerous rabble-rouser, while Tecumseh maintained that the crime had been organized by Black Hoof to make his village look bad. Obviously, discovering the truth was impossible in such an atmosphere of recrimination, and the only result of the conference was to exacerbate the break between Tecumseh and Black Hoof.

In 1808, Tecumseh and Tenskwatawa relocated their village at the confluence of the Wabash River and Tippecanoe Creek in Indiana, on a tract of land that had been offered them by the Kickapoo and Potawatomi tribes. The new site was more fertile, more accessible to friendly tribes, and further away from the American settlements. Construction immediately began on the new, bigger village that the Americans quickly named Prophetstown.

Later in the year, Tecumseh, along with approximately 1,500 chiefs and warriors from other tribes, went secretly to Canada on the invitation of the governor-general's deputy, Francis Gore. Tecumseh informed the Canadians that he was the head of a new, intertribal federation representing all the western Indians and demanded to meet with someone of equal status. Gore met with Tecumseh and agreed to send supplies and ammunition to Prophetstown with the tacit understanding that Tecumseh's federation would ally itself with the British in any upcoming conflagration. Although Tecumseh had little love for the British, who had after all betrayed his people at Fallen Timbers, he liked the settlers and land purchases of the United States even less and in any case needed supplies for his large group of followers. While Tecumseh was clandestinely securing supplies from the British, Tenskwatawa was openly securing supplies from Harrison, who although not entirely trusting Tenskwatawa, felt the need to cultivate his goodwill.

During the summer of 1809, Tecumseh left Tenskwatawa at Prophetstown and went south to seek the support of the Foxes, Sacs, and Winnebagos for his Indian union. While he was away, Har-

rison sent a message to the chiefs of the tribes that held land along the Wabash River, asking them to meet with him at Fort Wayne, Indiana. One thousand Native Americans came and were told that their father in Washington wished to buy their land. Harrison claimed, with some truth, that the land had been over-hunted; he claimed with lesser veracity that it was therefore of no use to their tribes. The chiefs, many of whom had been bribed previously by Indian agents, signed the Treaty of Fort Wayne, which in exchange for more than 3 million acres of land, alloted these tribes a single payment in goods of $7,000 and a small annual subsidy, to be divided among them.

But Harrison's latest success soon turned sour. Native Americans opposed to the treaty, led by the returned Tecumseh, declared the land sale invalid, ominously pointing out that it was one thing to claim land and another thing entirely to enforce that claim. In addition, they threatened the lives of the chiefs who had signed the treaty, intimidating into silence most of the Indian leaders who Harrison wished to use to garner Indian support for the treaty. As word of the agreement spread and Tecumseh's supporters expressed their opposition, Native Americans became less and less cooperative with the U.S government, and tribes that had been quiet for the past 15 years began once again to attack white settlements.

In Prophetstown, things could not have been better. The harvest had been successful, supplies were brought in by

British Indian agents throughout the winter, and Tecumseh's trips to enlist the support of the various tribes had been extremely successful—thanks in a large part to the Treaty of Fort Wayne. But Harrison became quite alarmed at Tecumseh's activities, and the two scrimmaged verbally several times over the next two years. Tecumseh continuously insisted that the Treaty of Fort Wayne had to be rescinded and that Americans had to stay in their own territory if the United States wanted the support and cooperation of the western Indians. Harrison, by now convinced that Tecumseh, not Tenskwatawa, was the real troublemaker, retaliated with overt and explicit threats of war.

In the fall of 1811, Tecumseh headed off with a band of warriors to attempt to enlist the aid of the large tribes in the South—the Chickasaws, Choctaws, and Creeks. Afraid that Harrison might attack Prophetstown while he was gone, he tried to smooth matters with Harrison before he left, and he told Tenskwatawa not to do anything to provoke the governor. Unfortunately, his powers of persuasion did not work so well with the southern tribes, whose experience with the whites so far had been much less hostile than that of their northern brethren—in part because they were mostly farmers and were less dependent on vast tracts of land for their survival. Only the Creeks agreed to send a group of warriors north, and these were only to observe the situation. Tecumseh returned home in early January 1812— and discovered that Prophetstown had

been destroyed.

Just as Tecumseh had feared, Harrison had decided to strike the headquarters of the Indian coalition while their most competent military leader was gone and had rounded up approximately 1,000 militiamen from Kentucky and Indiana. His men were inexperienced in war, as was he—but the same was true of the men remaining at Prophetstown, and Tenskwatawa, who the inhabitants of Prophetstown looked to as a leader, vacillated between peace offerings and war threats as Harrison and his men approached. Finally, on November 6, Tenskwatawa gathered the warriors of Prophetstown and told them that the Great Spirit had visited him. The Great Spirit had said that the Prophetstown forces should strike Harrison's men before the next sunrise, when the darkness would confuse the soldiers. In addition, he, the Prophet, would stand on a knoll near the battlefield, working his magic to make the Indians immune to the white man's bullets. The warriors set out to surround Harrison's men.

Around four o'clock in the morning on November 7, a sentry's shot rang out in Harrison's camp, alerting the soldiers to the attack. The element of surprise lost, Tenskwatawa's men immediately opened fire on the Americans, taking a heavy toll on the American troops but suffering greatly when the soldiers returned fire. Both armies were undisciplined, and the conflict at times resembled a mob action, but Harrison proved a capable leader and kept his men engaged in the two-hour battle. Tensk-

Harrison leads his troops against the Native Americans in the battle of Tippecanoe. The lack of competent military leadership among the Indians resulted in their defeat, and the battle not only demolished Prophetstown but destroyed Tecumseh's pan-Indian alliance and Tenskwatawa's reputation as a leader.

watawa, on the other hand, was far removed from the fighting, working his ineffective magic. When dawn came, the Indian troops began to retreat, only to discover that Tenskwatawa had preceded them and was nowhere to be found. The Indians scattered, and Harrison's men entered and destroyed the abandoned Prophetstown.

Tecumseh's pan-Indian coalition had been all but destroyed. Tenskwatawa was captured by the troops he once com-

manded, and although he managed to keep his life, he was disgraced, his reputation as a prophet and a leader ruined. Tecumseh, nothing if not indefatigable, tried to sustain those who had stayed at Prophetstown by going to Canada and begging for food supplies. Amazingly, Tecumseh was able to put together a small coalition in the spring, regaining the support of the anti-American Potawatomis, Winnebagos, Foxes, and Sacs, but losing his Wyandot, Delaware, and

Miami forces—and most of his Shawnee supporters. It was obvious now that if his confederacy was to have any real impact on the American policy, it must have the support of the British.

Tecumseh went to Ontario, Canada, in late June to meet with the British and learned that the United States had declared war on Britain on June 18. Tecumseh immediately returned to Prophetstown to inform his followers of the situation and, leaving Tenskwatawa in charge of the new community, joined the British army at Fort Malden, on the Canadian side of Lake Erie. Upon being informed that a large American force was marching to Detroit, from where to invade Canada, Tecumseh sent messengers to a number of the northwestern tribes telling them to join him and the British in Fort Malden. Some of these tribes immediately joined him, some decided to wait and see how the British did, and some, including Black Hoof's Shawnees, joined forces with the Americans. Despite the split in Native American support, the British and their Native American allies defeated the American invasive force in a number of battles, and in August, the Americans surrendered the fort in Detroit. News of this success and of the British capture of Chicago brought more tribes to the British side.

Unfortunately, succeeding attacks on targets further inside American territory ended in defeat, and Harrison had his men destroy some villages to punish the Native Americans for aiding the British. As a result, the Winnebagos and the Kickapoos returned to their villages to wait out the war, ruining a plan of Tecumseh's to have Tenskwatawa lead them in an attack on the town of Vincennes, Indiana, where Harrison was living. Instead, Harrison's troops attacked and destroyed the new Prophetstown, and Tenskwatawa and his few followers were forced to move to a small camp up the Tippecanoe. Surrounded by hostile troops and running out of food, they decided to make their way to join Tecumseh in Canada.

Once Tenskwatawa reached Canada, he and Tecumseh made a final daring trip to the Wabash Valley in 1813 to recruit more followers. When they returned to Fort Malden, they found the British general Henry Proctor ready to attack the newly built Fort Meigs on the Maumee River in Ohio, which was to be used as the base of American operations to retake Detroit. Tecumseh and Tenskwatawa led approximately 1,200 Indians to Fort Meigs, emboldened by the British promise that if the Americans surrendered, the Indians could claim the Michigan Territory as their new homeland, and by the prospect of capturing the commander of the fort—William Henry Harrison. They failed to take the fort but succeeded in annihilating a large force that was coming to assist Harrison.

Ironically, this victory proved damaging to the British, as a number of their Native American allies believed that the enemy was now vanquished and returned home. But Harrison's troops at Fort Meigs had not been captured, only temporarily neutralized, and as the bat-

Arrogant and stubborn, British general Henry Proctor considered his Native American allies untutored savages who did not deserve his confidence or trust. Naturally, this attitude alienated many warriors, and Proctor lost much of his Indian support as he frittered away his early advantage in the War of 1812.

tles in Ohio continued, Procter's lack of tactical skill took a heavy toll on his troops. In addition, the military forces in western Canada were not properly supplied or reinforced by the British. As a direct result of this neglect, the British naval forces on Lake Erie were destroyed by the fledgling American navy, and the Americans gained control of Lake Erie.

Upon hearing of the naval defeat, Procter, fearing that an invasive force could easily surround and destroy his troops at Fort Malden, decided to retreat. Unfortunately, he did not see the value of telling his Native American allies his decision and simply had his men pack up the fort. Tecumseh and his fellow warriors, afraid of being betrayed and abandoned again by the British, protested heartily and finally forced Procter to hold a meeting with the Native American troops. Much to their dismay, Procter told them that he had decided to abandon Fort Malden and with it any chance the Native Americans had of driving the Americans from their land.

Tecumseh's response aptly summed up the warriors' feelings towards Procter's retreat: "We must compare our father's [Procter's] conduct to a fat dog that carries its tail on its back but, when affrightened, drops it between its legs and runs off." If the British were not willing to fight the Americans, Tecumseh continued, the Indians surely were.

> Father, *listen!* . . . Father, you have got
> the arms and ammunition which
> our great father [the British king] sent

> to his children. If you have an idea
> of going away, give them to us, and
> you may go and welcome! For us,
> our lives are in the hands of the Great
> Spirit. We are determined to defend
> our lands and, if it be his will, we wish
> to leave our bones upon them.

Procter finally held a lengthy private meeting with Tecumseh, explaining how vulnerable Fort Malden was and maintaining that he did in fact wish to defend western Canada against the American invasive forces but simply wanted to do so at a more strategic location. Tecumseh agreed to cooperate, but again stated that abandoning the fort before ascertaining the size of the invasive force was cowardice. (Tecumseh was later supported in this opinion by the British military command during their court-martial of Procter.)

During Procter's retreat, over a thousand warriors deserted, unwilling to fight under his timid command. Seemingly belying his assertion that he merely wished to retreat to more easily defensible ground, Procter kept his troops moving for fully a week. Finally, he agreed to face the Americans at a spot by the road running alongside the Thames River. The British and Indian forces, totaling 800 soldiers and warriors, were vastly outnumbered by the pursuing Americans, 3,000 strong and led by none other than Harrison.

On October 5, 1813, Procter's and Tecumseh's forces met with the American invaders. Harrison directed his forces to charge the British flank first,

The death of Tecumseh at the Battle of the Thames is rather fancifully portrayed in this lithograph. A number of people (many with political aspirations) took credit for killing the legendary warrior, and a wide variety of accounts exist in both Shawnee and white lore describing the circumstances of his death and the fate of his body. The truth will probably never be known.

This portrait of Tecumseh was drawn by French trader Pierre Le Dru and is supposedly the most accurate likeness of him. Tecumseh reportedly refused to sit for portraits, and many depictions of him are based on memory or on descriptions made by friends.

and the British lines instantly crumpled and retreated, Procter leading the way. In contrast, the Native Americans fought doggedly, but they were hopelessly outnumbered and were forced to retreat, leaving their casualties on the battlefield to be retrieved later and buried during the long journey back to their villages. Among those casualties—as he had predicted to his followers the previous night—was the 44-year-old Tecumseh.

Despite some sporadic attempts at resistance by his followers, Tecumseh's death marked the end of organized Native American resistance in the Old Northwest. It also marked the end of any leadership possibilities for Tenskwatawa, who eventually moved to a home on the Missouri River near what is today Kansas City. He became something of a tourist attraction until his death in 1837, being interviewed and photographed by whites eager to meet one of the last dangerous Indians. Tecumseh's rival, Black Hoof, died in 1832, and his Shawnees were rewarded for their loyalty to the United States by being removed to reservations west of the Mississippi that same year. (In contrast to their earlier attempts to assimilate, these Shawnees actively resisted American cultural influences, refusing to learn English or send their children to white schools.)

Tecumseh's warnings about the threat the whites posed to the Native Americans proved truer than even he could imagine. But his portrait hangs in so many Shawnee homes today not so much for his predictions as for his willingness to stand up to the whites and brilliantly defend his culture, his land, and his people. Numerous legends have cropped up around Tecumseh's life, describing a veritable god among men with superhuman strength, amazing magical powers, and saintlike compassion. But while some of the stories are no doubt exaggerated, it cannot be denied that Tecumseh was, in the words of Bill Gilbert, "a hero, a noble man of nature, and one who was right." ▲

An elderly Shawnee woman works at an upright loom in this photograph, taken in 1970. Although the Shawnees have been forced to give up their historic lands, they have been remarkably successful in preserving their unique culture.

NOWHERE
LEFT
TO
GO

The history of the Shawnees after the death of Tecumseh can be compared to their earliest known history, when they migrated in small bands from one area to the next. The Shawnees would ultimately split into three independent tribes, the Absentee Shawnees, the Loyal or Cherokee Shawnees, and the Eastern Shawnees. But the primary difference between early and modern Shawnee history is that while in their early history they were free to choose where they wanted to go, after the end of the War of 1812, their activities were controlled by the government of the United States.

Soon after Britain's defeat, the U.S. government took 2 million acres of land belonging to the Northwest Indians, offering them a modest sum of money in exchange. There were no negotiations—the United States simply offered what it

considered an appropriate price, and the Native Americans were compelled to agree. Thanks to the military and political weakness of the Native Americans, the U.S. government was able to abandon any but the most transparent pretense of fair treatment in its drive to obtain new lands for settlement, and Native American land holdings quickly dwindled. This aggressive U.S. territorial expansion reached new lows of brutality with the presidency of Andrew Jackson, who proposed that all the Native Americans should simply be forced out of the area east of the Mississippi River. Congress enacted the Indian Removal Act into law on May 28, 1830.

A large group of Black Hoof's Shawnees in Ohio preemptively departed and joined the Shawnees in Missouri immediately after the War of 1812. Relations

99

between the two bands were tense—in a sense, neither side had forgotten the pain caused by the tribe's division during the American Revolutionary War—and in 1822, most of the old peace faction moved to eastern Texas, at the time a part of Mexico, and joined a multitribe group of Native Americans led primarily by Cherokees. The Mexican government had promised these Native Americans a tract of land, but the promise was an empty one; consequently, they supported the Texas independence movement. They were well-treated by the first president of the Texas Republic, Sam Houston (himself an adopted Cherokee), but he was unable to secure them a grant of land. Houston's successor, Mirabeau Lamar, was a notorious Indian hater who provoked the Native Americans into battle, defeated their forces, and forced them to leave Texas in 1839. The Shawnees separated from the other tribes and moved on to Oklahoma, settling on the Canadian River and forming the nucleus of what would be recognized in 1854 as the Absentee Shawnee (so called because they were absent from certain treaty negotiations made between the United States and a group of Kansas Shawnees).

The remainder of the Missouri Shawnees, called the Black Bob band, lost their Missouri land in 1825, when the U.S. government established a reservation for them in Kansas. They were joined in Kansas in 1832 by a number of Ohio Shawnees who had been allowed to remain east of the Mississippi until Black Hoof's death—the nucleus of the Loyal Shawnees. Relations between the Loyal Shawnees and the Black Bob band were troubled, in part because the Black Bob band had wanted to move to Oklahoma, and a large group of Black Bob Shawnees joined the Absentee tribe there in 1846. In 1854, the Kansas Shawnees were forced to sign a treaty with the U.S. government in which they were granted allotments of 200 acres of land to each individual tribal member—a policy in flagrant and deliberate opposition to traditional Shawnee group ownership of land. While some members of the tribe accepted the idea of individual allotments, the majority determined to act as communal owners of the reserve.

Events in Kansas took a violent turn when the American Civil War was declared. The vast majority of Shawnees were pro-Union, and many Shawnee men enlisted in the Union army during the Civil War, some as members of a Delaware and Shawnee company. As a result, Confederate guerrillas from Missouri frequently terrorized the Shawnee community in Kansas. Meanwhile, the pro-Union Absentee Shawnees in Oklahoma were harassed by their pro-Confederacy Creek neighbors. Fearful of Confederate attacks, the Absentee Shawnees fled Oklahoma, finding shelter with the Kansas Shawnees.

When the war was over, the Absentee tribe members returned to Oklahoma, only to discover that they had had no legal claim to their land and that tracts of it had been turned over to the Potawatomis as a reservation. The land situation worsened when, in 1869, the

SIWINOWE
Kesibwi.

·PALAKO WAHOSTOTA NAKOTE KESIBO.—WISELIBI, 1841.

J. LYKINS EDITOR.   **NOVEMBER, 1841.**   BAPTIST MISSION PRESS

SIEIWINOWEAKWA Nekinate, Sakimeki pahe eawibakeace kekesibomwi. Owanoke neketasbitolapa, kwakwekeaphe keahowaselapwipwi nawakwa noke wibakeata. Skiti ketalalatimolapwi howase lisimimowa, chena manwe laniwawewa.

           Eieiwekeati.

Hopakekiliwewa Tapalamalikwa Siwinowitowatota.

Siwinwike sakimeki laniwawe palako peace msaloke, hoaenoke miti. Mositiwe tipapakecike peace laniwaweke. Hotipenekeke pilohe makekobeke ksikea miti likomiwile Tapalamewalece. Hoaenoke milakhe Howase Eawekitake ealitowawice litowacile. Skiti cieike wieikotikke mosi nakote weponiniwi. Eawekitake piese keali netiwike eone wieioce namotake wieace mankwitoke. Cieike pwiei ponikke eomi eawekitake tipapakecike pipambake. Kekikikeake ma__ wise hikwalamikwa Tapalamalikwa chena wise nieabiwbake ketasetahawanani. Tapalamalikwa hewi; tbwalani selaniwake wanakisecke kokwalikwise walaniwaweke pwicinakisecke, wahiskime hikeebake.

malikwa palowe hoce helipimihe wanita belece; pieakwi honinotiwihe eamimitomakoce wabape laniwawelece.

Elane easelaniwawece eahowaselapwi hakoce Tapalamalikwa wise howase nhilwalamakoce matalamakoce otilalamile.

Hiwekitiwe elane pocelakho skota, chena miti einapobo?

Hinakote mkitawiloke eipamba, chena miti einapobo?

Ene eiski weabi neahiti milikwihe wace kilakoce wewile tihipelece, kokwanabi kice wawesihile miti eibibieikebe.

Ene easeliweti nahilwiki ocicilikomile, wahmeilat hile.

Lapwiti okwebemi wiwaselapwile, obile pieakwi wahitabeti okwebemi, mimicelapwile hokeale.

Sikealatiki pakekilolatewa nhilwiki osekealamile ocicilikomile.

Nieiswalatiki kelike laniwawewa waketamibewe;

Ealalatike ease kitanobota hipa__ eamace kitamoce miti hotinikiti.

Wanitabeti hocieieikitoti otase__awa waki lapwiwelane mieokwice eisetaha.

The *Shawnee Sun,* a newspaper printed by the Baptist Mission Press in 1841. Despite the pressure to assimilate into white American culture, the Shawnees (especially the Absentee Shawnees) became notorious for their unwillingness to give up their traditions, although many did adopt customs they found useful, such as literacy.

Kansas Shawnees were forced to move to Oklahoma, and the remaining members of the Black Bob band joined the Absentee Shawnees, increasing their land needs. Finally in 1872, the disputed lands were officially granted to the Absentee Shawnees.

But problems were still to come. A land allotment disagreement similar to the one in Kansas in 1854 split the Absentee Shawnees in 1875. While more accomodationist members accepted the land allotments, conservative members refused and the next year moved onto a nearby Kickapoo reservation until the U.S. Army forced them back in 1886. By this time, the Absentee Shawnees had become more embittered over the allotment policy, and a group of land speculators, seeing an opportunity to obtain Shawnee land, suggested that they give up their Oklahoma reservation and move to Mexico, where they would be free from the pressures of white settlement. The majority of the Absentee Shawnees stayed on the reservation, but leaders of a conservative Shawnee faction (including Wapameepo, called Big Jim by the whites, a militant activist and grandson of Tecumseh) decided that they could no longer tolerate the United States and departed for Mexico in 1900. Unfortunately, they reached their destination just as a smallpox epidemic hit, and all but two died. Although the fate of this faction was undeniably tragic, it did have the positive result of effectively ending any willingness of the Absentee Shawnees to cooperate with the often dishonest land speculators. Today 2,800

Absentee Shawnees live in Oklahoma, and they are one of the most culturally conservative Native American tribes in existence.

When the Kansas Shawnees who were originally a part of Black Hoof's tribe were forced to move to Oklahoma in 1869, they did not choose to join the Absentee Shawnees, as did the Black Bob band. Instead, they were recognized as a separate tribe and were assigned a hefty chunk of Cherokee land by the U.S. government as a way of rewarding them for their pro-Union sympathies during the Civil War (and not incidentally, to punish the pro-Confederacy Cherokees). In order to obtain the Cherokee land, the Loyal Shawnees—who had been making strong efforts to reclaim their traditional culture, which had been eroded as a result of Black Hoof's assimilationist policies—were required to give up much of their traditional culture and political organization. They are in the process today of carving a stronger identity for themselves.

A third group of Shawnees, who lived in a mixed Seneca and Shawnee village in Lewiston, Ohio, were removed directly to a reservation in northeastern Oklahoma in 1831. These Shawnees separated from the Senecas in 1867, taking the name of the Eastern Shawnees, and eventually organized themselves as the Eastern Shawnee Tribe in 1940. They have given up more of their traditional culture than any of the other Shawnee groups and most do not know the Shawnee language. They have approximately 1,550 tribal members, and anyone who

The grandson of Tecumseh, known as Wapameepto ("Gives Light as He Walks") by the Shawnees and as Big Jim by the whites, was a militantly conservative Shawnee leader who refused to farm or accept allotments despite the pressure put on him by the U.S. government. This portrait was taken approximately five years before he died.

can prove direct descendancy from the 280 members alive when the Eastern Shawnees became a federally recognized tribe can join. Their tribal complex, located in West Seneca, Oklahoma, consists of an administration office, a community building, and a bingo hall, which seats 750 people and employs 44.

All three Shawnee tribes have made extensive efforts to save or reclaim their culture. While many other tribes in Oklahoma have completely forgotten their traditional ceremonies, the Shawnees—despite the fact that many of them are now Baptist—still know their complete annual cycle of ceremonial dances, albeit in what is probably an eroded form. Shawnee ceremonial grounds still exist, and one located next to some ball fields in Whiteoak, Oklahoma, serves both the Loyal and the Absentee tribes. Although the ambience at these ceremonial grounds is reminiscent of ancient times when tribe members gathered to celebrate, the cars, pickup trucks, and campers parked around the grounds are a visible reminder that the Shawnees are a part of modern American society.

A newly designed tribal flag is unfurled by the chairman of the Absentee Shawnee tribal business committee, Danny Little Axe (left), and the flag's designer, Leroy White, in this 1974 photograph.

Modern Shawnee warriors—who served honorably in both world wars, the Korean War, and Vietnam—are respected in a traditional fashion, playing prominent roles in the War Dance that is still held each August by the Absentee Shawnees at the Little River, Oklahoma, ceremonial ground. Modern Shawnee chiefs have certain ritual functions but no political authority; instead, tribal councils conduct affairs in all three Shawnee tribes. Shawnee women are given a high position in their social and religious system today just as they were centuries ago. If women have the inclination, they hunt and fish, while men often tend children, prepare meals, and sew clothing.

Much of Shawnee craftwork today reflects the influence of other tribes. Shawnee women excel in beadwork and ribbonwork, and the men make drumsticks, peyote gourds, and staffs for their ceremonial costumes. A few of the women still make classic Shawnee moccasins as well as hatbands, belts, buckskin and cloth leggings, ribbon shirts, women's blouses, and women's hair ornaments that are distinctively Shawnee. A number of traditional Shawnee crafts are no longer made, however. Basket weaving died out in the 1930s, pottery making died out before the turn of the century, and hide tanning, although still in existence, is practiced very little today.

Most Shawnees today are of mixed divisional descent, and quite a few are of mixed tribal or racial descent as well.

Many Eastern and Loyal Shawnees share Oklahoma Seneca/Cayuga, Delaware, and Quapaw blood, while many Absentee Shawnees are also part Creek, Yuchi, Delaware, and Caddo.

Modern Shawnees live in two worlds, a mix of contemporary American society and traditional Shawnee culture. They raise cattle and work in trades or professions. They have small families. They live in contemporary American housing, and when Shawnee children are asked to draw the housing of their ancestors, they draw the tipis typical of the plains tribes. Almost all Shawnees speak English, and most Shawnees under 20 do not speak Shawnee—a situation elderly members of the Absentee tribe began to rectify in 1993 by inaugurating a program to teach children Shawnee. Compared to other tribes, the Shawnees are generally well-off economically, and they are one of the best-housed tribes in Oklahoma.

The Shawnees still rely on federal grants for support, however. Like the many other Native American tribes, they have faced astounding rates of poverty, disease, and alcoholism in their communities. But Shawnee leaders are determined to attain self-sufficiency for their tribes. This resolution was perhaps best stated by the late Eastern Shawnee chief Thomas A. Captain who wrote: "As your chief I refuse to live in the past. We have young Shawnee children growing up, and I pray to God that in time the Shawnee Nation can assist its own people." ▲

BIBLIOGRAPHY

Clark, Jerry E. *The Shawnee*. Lexington: University Press of Kentucky, 1977.

Clifton, James A. *Star Woman and Other Shawnee Tales*. Lanham, MD: University Press of America, 1984.

Cwiklik, Robert. *Tecumseh*. New York: Chelsea House, 1993.

Eckert, Allan W. *A Sorrow in Our Heart*. New York: Bantam Books, 1993.

Edmunds, R. David. *The Shawnee Prophet*. Lincoln: University of Nebraska Press, 1983.

———. *Tecumseh and the Quest for Indian Leadership*. Boston: Little, Brown, 1984.

Gilbert, Bill. *God Gave Us This Country: Tekamthi and the First American Civil War*. New York: Atheneum, 1989.

Harvey, Henry, ed. *History of the Shawnee Indians, from the Year 1681 to 1854*. 1855. Reprint. New York: Kraus Reprint, 1971.

Howard, James H. *Shawnee! The Ceremonialism of a Native American Tribe and Its Cultural Background*. Athens: Ohio University Press, 1981.

Trigger, Bruce G., ed. *Handbook of North American Indians*. Vol. 15, *The Northeast*. Washington, D.C.: Smithsonian Institution Press, 1978.

THE SHAWNEE AT A GLANCE

TRIBE   *Shawnee*
CULTURE AREA   *Northeast*
GEOGRAPHY   *Upper Midwest*
LINGUISTIC FAMILY   *Algonquian*
CURRENT POPULATION   *Approximately 12,350*
FEDERAL STATUS   *Recognized as the Absentee Shawnee, the Loyal or Cherokee Shawnee, and the Eastern Shawnee. Reservations in Oklahoma*

GLOSSARY

agent A person appointed by the Bureau of Indian Affairs to supervise U.S. government programs on a reservation and/or in a specific region.

allotment A U.S. government policy that broke up tribally owned reservations by assigning individual farms and ranches to Native Americans. Allotment was intended as much to discourage traditional communal activities as to encourage private farming and assimilate Indians into mainstream American life.

annuity Money or goods paid yearly or at a regular interval.

anthropologist A scientist who studies human beings and their culture.

anthropomorphic Described or thought of as having a human form or human attributes.

archaeologist A scientist who studies the material remains of past human cultures.

assimilation Changing one group's culture to accommodate a more dominant group.

Bureau of Indian Affairs (BIA) A federal government agency, now within the Department of the Interior, founded to manage relations with Native American tribes.

clan A multigenerational group having a shared identity, organization, and property based on belief in their descent from a common ancestor.

confederacy A union of related tribes or nations that functions as a political, military, or economic unit.

culture The learned behavior of humans; nonbiological, socially taught activities; the way of life of a group of people.

gauntlet A double row of men holding weapons to hit an individual made to run between them.

Indian Removal Act Legislation signed by President Andrew Jackson in 1830 that required many Indian tribes to relinquish their land in the East and move west of the Mississippi River.

Kokumthena The most important figure in the Shawnee religion, who created the world and will someday end it.

mishaami A Shawnee division's sacred bundle, containing holy objects considered crucial to the success of the tribe.

mission A center founded by advocates of a religion (particularly Christianity) to try and convert the nonbelievers to their faith.

msikamelwi A large wooden council house at the center of a Shawnee village.

nomadic Moving from place to place, often depending on the season or food supply, and establishing only temporary camps.

patrilinear Tracing descent through the father's side of the family.

peace chief A hereditary position that involves civil responsibilities such as organizing rituals, appointing people to ritual offices, and approving a decision to go to war.

priest-shaman A religious leader who acts as a healer, counselor, and diviner and who handles the mishaami.

reparations Compensation for damages.

reservation A tract of land retained by Indians for their own occupation and use.

sovereignty Freedom from external control.

treaty A contract negotiated between nations that deals with the cessation of military action, the surrender of political independence, the establishment of boundaries, the terms of land sales, and related matters.

tribe A society consisting of several separate communities united by kinship, culture, language, and other social institutions, including clans, religious organizations, and warrior societies.

war chief A respected warrior chosen to plan and lead war expeditions and to uphold the village laws.

wegiwa A Shawnee home, made of tapered wood poles lashed together and covered with animal skins or tree bark.

INDEX

PICTURE CREDITS

JANET HUBBARD-BROWN has a B.A. in Modern Humanities from New York University and is the author of three nonfiction books, including *The Mohawk* in Chelsea House's JUNIOR LIBRARY OF AMERICAN INDIANS series, and five historical mysteries for children. She lives with her husband and two children in Vermont, where she has just finished work on a CD-ROM murder mystery.